# Tibetan Mandala

Art and Practice

# Tibetan Mandala

## Art and Practice

## The Wheel of Time

Edited by
Sylvie Crossman and Jean-Pierre Barou

KONECKY&KONECKY

Konecky & Konecky
72 Ayers Point Rd.
Old Saybrook, CT 06475

This work translated from the French by Rosetta Translations.

ISBN: 1-56852-473-0


Jacket illustrations:
Front panel: Collection Art sans Frontières
Back panel: Photographs Gian Franco Lunardo

Printed and bound in China

# Contents

The monastery of Samyé, eighth century, the first
monastery built in Tibet. Its architecture was
planned as a mandala.

# The Universality of Form

Jean-Pierre Barou

In 1909 in Munich, the Russian painter Wassily Kandinsky was becoming interested in abstract art. But he was hesitant. Although "emptiness" had always fascinated him, he was afraid that without any references to reality, his paintings might, as he put it, resemble patterns on a tie or a rug. If the picture did not resemble anything, having been reduced to a color here and another there, how could it express the inner life without lapsing into nothingness or arbitrariness?

Kandinsky was to find the answer to his questions in India and Tibet. Here was the intoxication of an artist on the threshold of perhaps the most daring artistic challenge of the twentieth century. For Kandinsky the solution would lie on the Himalayan slopes where thought had freed itself from the burden of appearances. This influence has been overlooked by art historians. In fact, modern art has undergone a two-pronged development: Oceania and Africa were sources of inspiration for Matisse, Picasso, the Fauves, and the Cubists, while India and Tibet guided Kandinsky, Mondrian, Malevich, and Klee towards abstraction.

The way towards abstract art was paved by Helena P. Blavatsky who was born in Dnepropetrovsk in 1831. She has been excluded from the mainstream of Western thought. Her claims to supernatural powers could not be taken seriously.

Gandhi, however, in his memoirs pays homage to the "Russian Sphinx" as she was known. It was on her advice that, while studying in London, he read in the original the *Bhagavad gita*, the great national poem that in essence sums up the entire religious thought and philosophy of India. Madame Blavatsky had just published *The Key to Theosophy*. Gandhi wrote that this book freed him from the idea was taught by the missionaries, that Hinduism was merely popular superstition.[1]

1. *Gandhi's Autobiography: The Story of My Experiments with Truth*, Washington D.C., 1948

Wassily Kandinsky, *Untitled*, (first abstract watercolor) 1913,*
49.60 x 64.80 cm, Centre Georges Pompidou, Musée National
d'Art Moderne, Paris. (© ADAGP, Paris 1995.)

* Kandinsky dated this work 1910. This fact was contested by art historians
after his death and that of his wife.

Helena Blavatsky had many faults, but they did not include that of writing about India without going there. She traveled to India three times, in 1855, in about 1876 and again in 1879. She even tried to enter Tibet, which was a closed country at the time. These were not easy journeys, since India was an integral part of the British Empire and the authorities disapproved of Blavatsky's encouraging the native population to preserve "their religion and not to abandon it without proof of its unworthiness."

In a note dating from 1875, she wrote: "People in Europe and America should learn about India's wisdom, its philosophy, and its achievements. The British must be persuaded to respect the indigenous population of India and Tibet more than they do at present."[2] She was trying to build a bridge between the East and the West.

## Kandinsky's Color Circle

Kandinsky himself discovered Blavatsky in about 1909—her book on theosophy had appeared in Germany in 1907. He wrote: "There is an increasing number people who have lost all hope in the methods of materialistic science regarding any questions dealing with 'non-matter' or with matter that is not accessible to the senses. And like art, which turns to the primitive, these people look for guidance to almost forgotten eras and their methods. But these methods are in fact still used by certain peoples... including those of India, for instance... Madame H. P. Blavatsky, who spent many years in India, was undoubtedly the first to establish a firm link between these 'savages' and our culture."[3] Kandinsky borrowed directly from Blavatsky's writings.

He now knew that he had been mistaken. A painting can abandon representation so long as it addresses the mind of the viewer and not only the eye. The eye is a window that opens onto a network of nerves leading to the brain. The colors used by the "peoples" mentioned by Blavatsky[4] address the hidden areas of the mind, and they appeal to intuition: but this is not the intuition of the philosophers of "becoming," such as Bergson and Croce, for whom it is a foreshadowing that will eventually be confirmed by logic. India and its peoples speak of another intuition, far beyond reason, outside the world of senses, an intuition that is the only way to true knowledge.

Kandinsky, Russian by birth but more Oriental than Slavic, as his contemporaries pointed out,[5] and who saw himself as a reincarnation of a Chinese wise man, created a remarkable "color circle" which he deconstructed into three pairs, yellow-blue, red-green, and orange-violet. Two poles, black and white, frame the circle. It was, he said, "the life of simple colors between birth and death."

The "close relationship between the color circle as he defined it and the concept of the mandala" was noted by Philippe Sers, an expert on Kandinsky. What do the colors and symbols in a Tibetan mandala address if not the mind of the viewer looking at it?

Kandinsky continued: "If one allows blue to influence the soul... it will draw man towards the infinite, arousing in him a nostalgia for the Pure and the ultimate supersensibility;" "absolute green is the most restful color

2. We have borrowed from the work of Noël Richard-Nafarre, *Helena P. Blavatsky ou la Réponse du Sphinx*, 1991

3. Wassily Kandinsky, *Concerning the Spiritual in Art*, New York, 1946.

4. Volume VI of *The Secret Doctrine*, of Helena P. Blavatsky, contains many references to the symbolism of colors.

5. Suzanne Markos-Ney in particular has emphasized how Kandinsky was already an "oriental" in his way of speaking and using metaphor: in Nina Kandinsky, *Kandinsky und ich*, Munich, 1976.

there is…; it asks for nothing, it attracts nothing;" "white also influences our soul (psyche) like a deep silence, absolute within us."

Painting a picture is thus returning to the manipulation of color with the objective of "refining the human soul." Neither Kandinsky, Mondrian, Malevich, nor Klee ever believed in the virtues of historical materialism that was developing at the time. On the contrary, they denounced the mechanization and dehumanization of modern times in which the individual was only a link in a chain, and from the very start they condemned the totalitarian systems that would come to dominate Germany and Russia.

In 1911 in Amsterdam, Mondrian followed the same path. He was a member of the Theosophical Society, he was an avid reader of the works of Blavatsky, and he meditated in the lotus position. Throughout his life he kept a photograph of the theosophist with him. His own abstract paintings were inspired by the esoteric geometry described by the Society's founder.

In Moscow, Malevich, the creator of *Black Square on a White Ground*, another giant step along the road of abstraction, regularly read the magazine *Vestnik Teosofii*, the Muscovite mouthpiece of theosophy. His "suprematist" paintings led to his arrest by the authorities. His aim was to reach the deeper being concealed behind appearances and, on the subject of "intuitive consciousness"[6] he wrote these crucial words: "What an absurd doctrine to believe that our eyes know how to see!"

The convergence in the gestures and thoughts of the future abstract artists is remarkable. It was Klee, now in Bern, who wrote in his journal "In moments of clarity, I sometimes reflect upon twelve years of the inner development of my own self. First the diminished self, the heavily blinkered self (the egocentric self), then the disappearance of the blinkers and the self, and now little by little a self without blinkers (the divine self)."

## Matisse: Painting as a "Cerebral Sedative"

Yet neither Kandinsky, nor Mondrian, Malevich nor Klee was ever initiated into the mysteries of the mandala proper, to this labyrinth which, if followed correctly, would rid the "ego" of any excess, and lead one beyond appearances to Absolute Being—the essence, the knowledge—that shines in its centre.

This was even more true of Matisse who in 1908 declared that colors acted like a "cerebral sedative." Apollinaire indeed considered Kandinsky to be a "disciple" of Matisse. One day in 1948, Matisse strangely remarked to Picasso, who was taken aback to see him decorating the chapel at Vence, "I don't know whether I am a believer or not. Perhaps I am a Buddhist!"[7]

The lessons of India, its visions unburdened by realism, continued to inspire these artists. For all of them, what colors were "saying" was

6. See Jean-Pierre Barou, *L'Œil pensé, essai sur les arts primitifs contemporains*, Editions Balland, Paris, 1993.

7. Henri Matisse, *Matisse on Art*, ed. by Jack Flam, New York, 1973.

beyond words, and gradually infiltrated their work. Painting was no longer simply an aesthetic project, it had assumed a "moral" dimension, as an active support for meditation. As Kandinsky explained, "An artistic fraud will result in a series of unhappy consequences." This is reminiscent of the Tibetan masters for whom the slightest error in the design of a mandala, such as a missing line, an irregular circle, or an imperfect color, could threaten the life not only of the artist but also of the person looking at it.

1916. On the shores of Lake Zurich, the psychiatrist Carl Gustav Jung had broken off all relations with Freud and was in a state of crisis. Holding a notebook in his hand, he kept finding that his pencil invariably moved towards the center of the page. He had just succeeded in bringing the "mandala" to the surface of his consciousness, although it was not until 1928, after he had seen those centered, circular paintings from India, that he called his own drawings "European mandalas."

He distanced himself from Freud's emphasis on "reason," a concept distrusted by creative people at the beginning of the century. Freud believed that psychoanalysis was entirely ruled by reason. Jung on the other hand suspected the existence of other laws could be discerned in painting, poetry, and the great religious myths of humanity. He did not fear the unconscious; he regarded it as a source of spiritual riches.

In any case he would never forget the "mandala" and was able to identify its many variations, as sources of healing and of "re-centering," in his patients' drawings.[8]

When the great Italian orientalist and Tibet expert Giuseppe Tucci arrived in Tibet in 1935, he paid tribute to Jung. Studying mandalas there, he remarked that this circle was indeed a "psycho-diagram."[9] Each of its colors reflected components of the human personality, the poisons blocking the way: white reflected ignorance, yellow pride, red lust, green jealousy

8. Jung was always careful to point out that the "European mandala" did not achieve the perfection or harmony of the "oriental mandala." Also, he believed that Helena Blavatsky's work gave too much consideration to the East, the risk being that of becoming a "pitiable imitator."

9. Giuseppe Tucci, *Theory and Practice of the Mandala*, New York, 1970.

Left:
Romio Hrestha,
contemporary Nepalese
painter, *The Shakyamuni
Buddha* (detail), 1993.
(Private collection.)

and blue-black anger. There was no doubt that this imagery was a support for learning and meditation. It helped the disciple, led by a "guru," to bring to light within the labyrinth of consciousness those "obscuring passions" that had to be driven out. The colors are points of reference, a system of signs, a carefully chosen grammar for reshaping the personality, as Tucci also noted, but on a higher plane, and after an initial process of "disintegration" and analysis had taken place.

As the century progressed, explorations grew bolder. Like other young men of the 1960s, John Blofeld, followed in the footsteps of the Indian masters. He was initiated into Buddhism, traveled extensively through Asia and immersed himself in the varieties of experience to be had there. He wrote that the use of mescaline, dear to twentieth-century writers, especially Malcolm Lowry and Henri Michaux, generated "in the remote corners of the mind not only abstract symbols corresponding very closely to Tibetan mandalas, but also creatures resembling the deities of the mandala."[10] And those who have known Blofeld point out the seriousness of this initiate.

10. John Blofeld, *The Tantric Mysticism of Tibet*, New York, 1970.

## Complex Techniques of Visualization

It is a remarkable fact that the oldest mandalas preserved by history date from the sixth century. For instance, there is a seal in the Metropolitan Museum of Art, New York, consisting of a center containing Shakyamuni, the founder of Buddhism, surrounded by eight bodhisattvas or "saints," and this seal is indeed from the sixth century.[11]

A heart in which a Buddha sits, surrounded by eight petals, each one bearing a deity: this is the image reproduced by all mandalas today.

11. Cf. Gilles Béguin, *Mandala, diagrammes ésotériques du Népal et du Tibet au musée Guimet*, Editions Findakly, Paris, 1993.

But according to Tibetan and Indian belief, the invention of this figure can be traced much further back, to the sixth century BC, to Shakyamuni himself, the historic Buddha. It was a year after reaching the state of Awakening that he designed this mandala, which he dedicated to the Master of Time, Kalachakra. His idea was to draw a path of colors that would retrace his own progression outside the world of phenomena and towards the state of Awakening.

Tibet is the chosen land of the mandala. Tibetan Buddhism attaches particular importance to the visualization techniques through which a colored symbol can imprint itself in the mind of the person practicing them, changing its course and even its nature. According to lama Anagarika Govinda, "an image or a symbol that has no effect is at best a decorative picture."[12] Kandinsky echoes this with his affirmation of the moral value of art: a picture is "bad" if its spiritual consequences or its "vibrations" are negative or have no effect. As for these symbols, the lama Govinda continues, far from being arbitrary expressions they are "spontaneous forms of expression emerging from the deepest regions of the human mind." The Jungian "archetypes"…

12. Anagarika Govinda, *Foundations of Tibetan Mysticism*, New York, 1974.

Imported from India, the "Kalachakra Mandala" or "Wheel of Time" has always been the object of an important cult in Tibet. It is often created as an ephemeral work of art using colored powders that are then scattered over the bodies of the faithful or into the waters of a river or stream. "Yes, I believe that one can interpret this mandala as being necessary in

Left:
"European mandala" created by a patient of Jung, who interpreted this figure as an expression of the conflict between nature and nurture. Collection C. G. Jung Institute, Zurich.

the twentieth century," pointed out Dagpo Rinpoche, the great Tibetan scholar and former professor at the Institute of Oriental Languages in Paris, from his house in the city's suburbs where he has found refuge since the 1960s.

The present Dalai Lama, Tenzin Gyatso, is the fourteenth in a line founded in the fifteenth century. He has shown particular interest in the Kalachakra Mandala. At the age of nineteen, in 1954, the young spiritual leader of the Tibetans since 1940 gave his first initiation into the Kalachakra at Lhasa before ten thousand people. Indeed, from the start the Kalachakra has never been taught to a single disciple but always to a group of at least twenty-five people. He repeated the initiation in 1957 when his country was invaded by communist China. He left Tibet in 1959 and went into exile at Dharamsala, a town in northern India. There in the hills he built a temple dedicated to Shakyamuni and another in homage to Kalachakra. In 1971, having resumed his teaching, he dreamed: "I realized that I was going to teach this many times. I believe that in my previous lives I had a special link with the Kalachakra."

He added that "the initiation to the Kalachakra is one of the most important in Buddhism because it takes everything into account: the body and the human mind, and the whole external aspect—cosmic and astrological."

Again time blurs. His words seem to echo those of the initiates (Klee called an abstract painter an "initiate") of the Western world rebelling against mechanization when he explains: "At the present time, the world is not guilty of a lack of technological and industrial development. What we lack today is a foundation on which to build harmony and mental and spiritual joy."

There is no doubt that the occupation of their own country by communist China has further convinced Tibetans that they have to intervene in this troubled world. Long ago their oracles had foretold these barbaric times and predicted that they would need to appeal to the Kalachakra for help.

# The Navajo Medicine Paintings

Eternal and universal. It is interesting to note the similarity between the Tibetan mandala and sand paintings in other continents, such as for instance the Navajo "medicine paintings" whose aim is also to help and heal. These too have a quaternary rhythm and a center. Like its Tibetan counterpart, the "Navajo mandala" is scattered over the patient or even on the ground. This painting is also produced without a model but in this case without tools. The Navajo medicine man takes some colored powder in the palm of his hand and lets it filter through his thumb and index finger to form a circle. There are day pictures, which must be completed before sunset, and night paintings, produced inside the house. A single word, *ikeah*, meaning "that which comes from the mind," describes all these works. There too it is said that simply looking at a sand painting can have a calming effect on the viewer. As Joe Ben Jr., a contemporary Navajo artist faithful to his people's tradition, explains: "The eye is the instrument through which healing will take place." Again "beauty" has a purpose. It is there to act and to save; it is no longer destined only for museums and the marketplace.

In Australia, the Aborigines use natural pigments and feathers to create ephemeral installations on the very surface of the desert, sometimes covering two or three acres. There again a geometric figure arising from the depths of time is dominant: a coil of concentric circles. Renewed periodically, these creations ensure the survival of fauna and flora. Nothing has been forgotten: even a simple fly near a vast salt lake in central Australia, Lake Eyre, has its annual ritual.[13]

The thread of the mandala continues to unwind. In Barcelona in 1994 the Dalai Lama gave his second initiation in Europe. Was it presumptuous on his part to suggest the possible use of this figure in fields hitherto reserved to science? To suggest that the mandala could help in cases of AIDS?

On reaching the higher levels, those who practice the Kalachakra "visualize," they picture its energies and its vital breaths, both male and female, in order to marshal them like an army. Kalachakra has three necks, three channels: red, white, and, in the center, blue, where everything is brought together.

In recent years Western medicine has also begun to appeal to the imagination of the patient, encouraging the use of visualization techniques to imagine his or her own immune systems in order to take control of them. An American radiologist in Texas, Carl Simonton, has gone so far as to suggest that cancer is the translation of mental defeat into the cellular system.[14]

The access to the supreme consciousness sometimes seems to rest on a "launching pad" formed by this body of assembled energies. At the end of his journey through the mandala, the Tibetan initiate appears indeed to

13. Faced with this diversity, the first ethnologists were doubtful. This almost microscopic sense of responsibility did not really match the idea that they were "primitives." On the subject of this same ritual of Australian survival and the moral rules that it implied, Freud in particular did not hide his skepticism in *Totem and Taboo*, a work particularly acerbic to the position of "natives." It was not until the following generation of researchers that this truth was admitted by the western scientific community. See A. P. Elkin, *The Australian Aborigines and How to Understand Them*, Sydney, Australia, 1938.

14. See Sylvie Crossman / Edouard Fenwick, *Californie, le nouvel âge*, Editions de Seuil, Points Actuels collection, Paris, 1983.

be propelled, leaving the bodily envelope and escaping from a world dominated by poisons to become an "empty form," empty in the sense in which infinity is empty. Thus he generates himself, he self-generates, he becomes Buddha!

Taking charge of one's self, of others, and of the world, the mandala implies this practice of "self-management" at all times. Yet it retains an exalted nature that in everyday life rejects degrading, exhausting work that can distract the human being from his objective, the conquest of consciousness. This may explain why thinkers such as why Simone Weil, philosopher of the working classes, Albert Camus who depicted man's condition of isolation in the world, and René Daumal, poet of the peaks and author of *Mount Analogue*, have felt so strongly attracted to Eastern religions.

The influence of Tibet on them, as on the masters of abstraction, remains secret and unknown.

But the "Wheel of time" silently moves on.

Left:
Joe Ben Jr., Navajo artist, "healing" painting, 1993. (Private collection.)

# Tibet
# The Kalachakra Mandala
# or
# The Wheel of Time

*The initiation to the Kalachakra is one of the most important in Buddhism because it takes everything into account: the body and the human mind, and the whole external aspect—cosmic and astrological. By its complete observance, it is possible to achieve Awakening in a single lifetime. We firmly believe in its power to reduce conflict and we believe it is capable of creating peace, peace of the spirit and therefore peace in the world.*

Tenzin Gyatso, the fourteenth Dalai Lama, 1993.

# One Palace, Five Levels

The "Wheel of Time" is a "divine palace" in which 722 deities reside. Right at its the center, on a lotus flower, is a Buddha: Kalachakra.

This palace has five floors or levels, represented by five squares superimposed on each other. This palace is a mandala, a support for teaching and meditation: 1) the body mandala, 2) the speech mandala, 3) the mind mandala, 4) the pristine consciousness mandala, 5) finally, in the center, with its lotus, the bliss mandala, the objective of this course of initiation.

This palace is inscribed within six large concentric circles, representing the universe.

According to Tibetan tradition the "Wheel of Time" is all-encompassing. It emphasizes the correspondences linking human beings with the outside world. Indeed one speaks of the "external Kalachakra," which covers astronomy, astrology and mathematics; the "internal Kalachakra," the structure of the human body and its system of energies; and the "alternate Kalachakra," the study and observance that lead from the ordinary state to the state of Enlightenment.

To make a Kalachakra is to promote peace in each person and on earth.

The colors represent the four cardinal points: black, the east; red, the south; yellow, the west; and white, the north. A fifth, green, adds rhythm to the pattern that even when produced on a flat surface with colored powders, appears like a three-dimensional image; thus the center of the lotus flower, right in the middle, is made up of five layers of superimposed colors that correspond to the five levels of the palace.

At this center, Kalachakra is represented by a blue *vajra*, the *vajra* ("diamond scepter" or "thunderbolt") being the emblem of Tibetan Buddhism.

The teaching of the Kalachakra always takes place at a full moon. Imbued with compassion, the fundamental virtue in Tibetan Buddhism, and guided by a master, the novices slowly mentally penetrate this palace by going round clockwise, having first presented themselves at the east gate of the body mandala.

To reach the central chamber is to join the Kalachakra (who has successfully followed this path), embracing his female partner Vishvamata in his arms. An orange-yellow dot, to the right of the blue *vajra*, represents Vishvamata. In Tibetan cosmology, Kalachakra is associated with the moon and Vishvamata with the sun. Their embrace symbolizes the union of compassion and absolute wisdom into which the faithful must dissolve in order to be purified and reborn beyond the world of phenomena, as an empty form, immutable, pure essence.

It is said that a simple glance at the Kalachakra Mandala can sow "seeds" in the mental development of the viewer that will mature and yield positive effects. It is also said that the brilliance of this mandala is a hundred times greater than that of the sun.

J.-P. B., S. C.

# 1. The Body Mandala

*This is the bottom level of the palace of Kalachakra. A total of 536 deities reside in this mandala.*

Forming the decorative frame, three bands, white, blue and black, in a blend of architecture and symbolism represent respectively a parapet to protect against the assault of blurring passions; a row of gutters to drain off the rainwater of this palace; and garlands of white pearls, symbolizing the virtues associated with the Buddha. They end in dots that stand for offerings: fans made of yak hair, mirrors, and bells.

Next comes a frieze of red and gold jewels.

This is followed by the *dhoenam*, white, forming four "L" shapes, the residence of the offering goddesses. These deities are side by side with geometric figures whose colors recall the constituent elements that make up the universe and whose shapes are active: the circle pacifies, the square increases energy tenfold, the arc of the circle is a sign of permission, and the triangle is a sign of accomplishment.

These are followed by five foundation walls, represented by five bands of color.

Then comes the *lhanam*, a white square, that accommodates other deities, 360 in number, corresponding to the 360 days of the Tibetan lunar year, out of the total of 536 deities in this mandala. They are supported by twelve animals symbolizing the twelve months of the year.

Finally there is a frame made up of four colored trapezoids. Four T-shaped doors lead into the mandala.

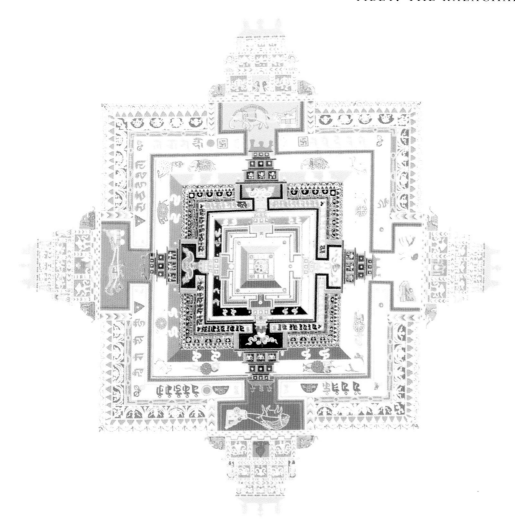

# 2. The Speech Mandala

*This is the second level of the palace. It refers to the virtues of the words of the Buddha delivering his teachings. 116 deities reside on this second level.*

As in the body mandala, the deities of the dhoenam of this second mandala are represented by "seed syllables," which are pure sounds able to cause the deity to appear in the mind of the disciple. It should be mentioned that *mantras*, Tibetan prayers, are made up of a succession of seed syllables, evoking truths that words cannot express.

Similarly, its foundation walls are made of five colored bands —yellow, white, red, black and green—and again, as in the body mandala, they symbolize the five faculties that make access to knowledge possible: wisdom, concentration, attention, effort, and trust. These bands also refer to the five major Buddhas of the Tibetan pantheon who, unlike the historical Buddha, are legendary characters. These are Akshobya, Amitabha, Amoghasiddhi, Ratnasambhava, and Vairocana.

The secondary deities in the *lhanam* are *yoginis*, that is, female ascetics in yoga poses.

The four trapezoids and their colors refer to the four faces of Kalachakra: the black face at the front is angry; the red on the left is exalted; the white on the right is peaceful; and the yellow at the back is fulfilled.

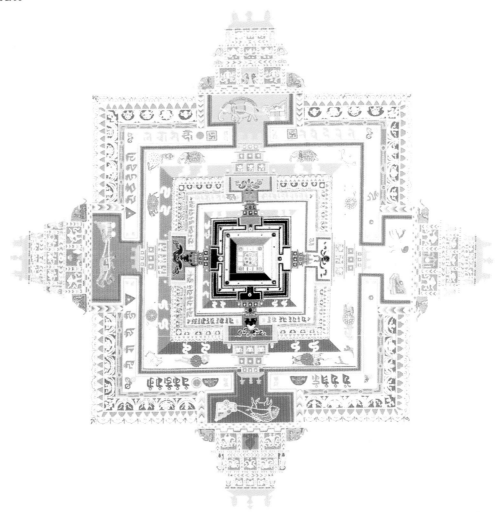

# 3. The Mind Mandala

*70 deities inhabit this third level of the palace of Kalachakra*

The structure is unchanged, but the decorative enclosure is reduced to three simple bands of color. Although invisible, the fans made of yak hair alleviate the burns of ignorance, the mirrors reflect the emptiness of all phenomena, and the bells echo the sound of emptiness.

The *dhoenam* contains the Four Noble Truths, the fruit of the first sermon of Shakyamuni, the historical Buddha. They are inscribed on either side of each of the four doors, in the shape of two half-moons.

The foundation walls consist of three bands instead of five: black, red, and white, which represent the three "Vehicles" or "Paths" of Buddhism: the "Lesser Vehicle" that appeared in the sixth century BC with Shakyamuni, the historical Buddha; the "Greater Vehicle" that stresses compassion and appeared in about the second century AD; and the "Diamond Vehicle," an offshoot of the "Greater Vehicle" that appeared in Tibet in the fifth–sixth century AD. Through this Vehicle one can reach Awakening in a single life. This Tibetan path encourages the artistic imagination—the mandalas—as a tool to reach Enlightenment or Absolute Truth.

The secondary deities in the *lhanam* are *bodhisattvas*. These beings on the path to Enlightenment delay their own Awakening and reincarnate themselves to help others towards this Awakening.

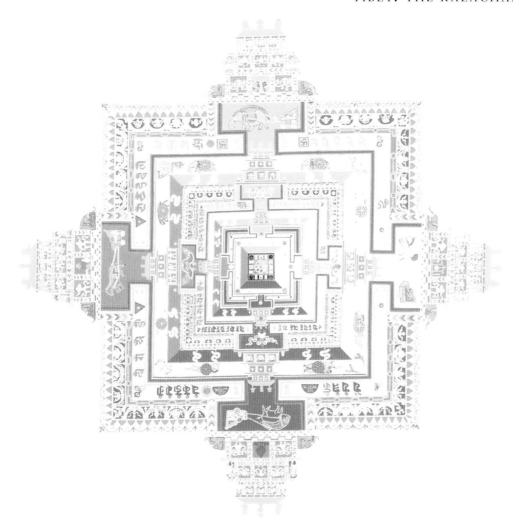

# 4. The Pristine Consciousness Mandala

*The mandala of "pristine consciousness," the fourth level of this palace, is hollowed out at its center by the "Great Bliss" mandala.*

Two blue lines mark the external boundary of this square. These are the foundation walls. Between these two bands, a chain of *vajras* evokes the indestructibility of the Awakened Mind.

Sixteeen black pillars, four in each direction, symbolize sixteen different categories of emptiness. These pillars mark the boundary of the sixteen chambers, eight of which (those facing the cardinal points and those at the corners) each contains a lotus flower with eight petals on which a pair of embracing deities rests in the same way that Kalachakra intimately embraces Vishvamata in the center of the palace. The other eight chambers each house a vase filled, it is said, with the purified substances of the body: the blood, the bone marrow, and the seminal fluid.

At this stage, the disciple, cleansed of the stains of the phenomenal life, is able to achieve the subtle, pristine consciousness.

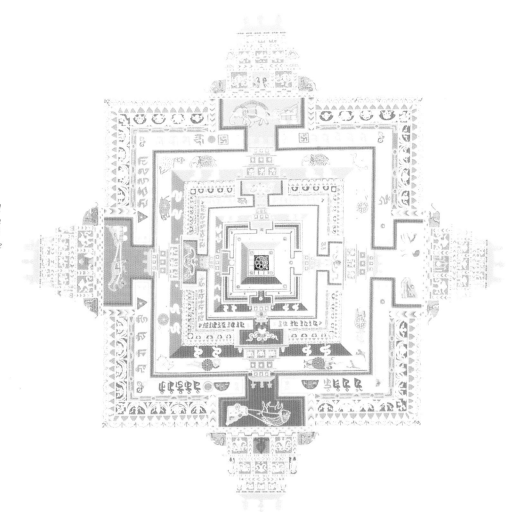

# 5. The Great Bliss Mandala

## *Entering "Happiness"*

This is the highest level of the palace; a lotus flower with eight petals is drawn inside this final square. At each corner, a colored dot refers to the qualities of the body, the word, the mind, and the consciousness of the Kalachakra. A *shakti*, a female deity, is seated on each petal. Kalachakra, symbolized by a blue *vajra*, is seated in the center of the lotus. Blue refers to immutability, this Buddha being here beyond time and becoming. He is inseparable from Vishvamata, his consort, who is represented by an orange-yellow dot placed on his right.

Two other pairs of Buddhas live in the center of this lotus flower: they are Akshobya and Vajrasattva, they too are in intimate embrace with their respective consorts, Prajnaparamita and Vajradhatvishvari.

The position of intimate embrace symbolizes the Awakening, that is, the union of compassion and absolute wisdom. At this stage the tantric initiate is supposed to consolidate all his energies, male and female, white and red, seminal and bloody, lunar and solar—Kalachakra being related to the Moon and Vishvamata to the sun—in the central channel that runs through the body from bottom to top. (Tibetan anatomy recognizes three of these channels, the other two being situated on either side of the central channel.)

The disciple can then slough off his original mortal shell and become an empty, immutable form, a pure essence, a Buddha himself.

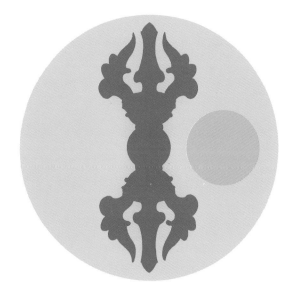

Left:
In the center of the wheel of time, Kalachakra, in the form of a blue *vajra*, is in intimate union with his consort, Vishvamata, a yellow-orange disc on the right. They rest on five layers of color (in order: green, white, red, blue, and yellow). Only the last, the yellow one, is visible.

# How to Choose your Mandala

Dagpo Rinpoche

Choosing a mandala is like choosing a partner. You must feel particularly drawn towards him, I mean, towards the person who occupies its center and who varies from one mandala to another. In fact each deity,[1] or at any rate the majority of them, has a mandala that is appropriate to him. One must therefore identify the bond that links us to one or another deity. In our past lives, we have accumulated *karma* (actions), we have experienced feelings and felt passions, and this has created in us a kind of affective landscape that, in our present life, guides us naturally towards certain shapes, towards certain beings, certain deities. A lama can help you in your search.

We know that we have found our deity when we experience a particular joy and feeling of peace in his presence. It is not that we are drawn to a particular feature but rather to the ensemble.

I know, it is perhaps a little difficult to understand this from the outside. I wonder how to explain it better. Well, for instance, when you are sad or when you are frightened, as soon as the picture of your deity appears, you will feel better and able to cope again. A person can have a special bond with several deities, as I do.

Having made this choice, you will know which mandala to work and meditate with.

1. Deity: There are two kinds of deities, the "worldly deities," that evolve in our world and that can be defined as kinds of spirits or states of mind. Then there are the "deities beyond the world," which we are concerned with here. These are the forms and emanations taken either by the historic Buddha, or other buddhas, according to the temperament of each disciple, with the aim of expounding the teaching in the most efficacious manner.

# The Practice of the Mandala

Sylvie Crossman / Jean-Pierre Barou

An artistic and philosophical training of at least three years is required before being allowed to construct an ephemeral Kalachakra or "Wheel of Time" mandala in sand. Although there are Kalachakra mandalas that are carved or painted, or sometimes even only pictured in the mind, the most perfect ritual calls for a Kalachakra mandala produced with colored powders so that it can ultimately be scattered on the devotee and mixed with the earth.

Four monks carry out the work, using rulers, a compass, and string. First they trace a diagram on a horizontal support, placed waist-high, painted in blue or dark red: blue, like the center of the mandala, dark red, like the monks' habits. Even at this stage, great precautions are taken, rather similar to those of a surgeon carrying out an operation. The slightest mistake in drawing this centuries-old diagram of this Wheel, intended to bring peace to earth, would make it ineffective. The rulers, compass, and string will have been purified in advance. This string is impregnated with powder and used to draw the straight lines.

The first two lines are perpendicular to each other, one aligned east-west and the other north-south. Their point of intersection determines the center of the future mandala. The next two lines are two diagonals through the center point defining eight equal parts.

On these straight lines that form a star, three squares are superimposed on each other, the second square being half the size of the first, and the third half the size of the second.

Two other squares are drawn in the center. In the smaller one, a monk draws the outline of a lotus flower, consisting of a center and eight petals. Around this stylized lotus flower a whole plan takes shape, spreads and becomes clearer; T-shaped doors are placed on the sides of the first three squares. The whole drawing is enclosed within six large outer circles—the universe.

After a purification ceremony has taken place, the time to add color arrives.

One monk climbs onto the support. The risk of setting foot on such a sacred work is great. Would one tread on a drawing of Christ? That would

Opposite page:
Kalachakra in intimate union with Vishvamata, a figurative illustration on contemporary *thangka*. Collection Art Sans Frontières.

29

Right:
Using ruler and compass,
the monks draw the outline
of the base of the mandala,
the foundations of this
"palace."

be likerenouncing one's vows. The monk must control his mind by using a technique of "visualization," imagining that the lines of the diagram are higher than they appear, and that they are detached from the table so that he is no longer treading on them.

He sits down in the "eastern" quarter of the diagram. Instead of a brush he uses a long metal open-ended cone, known as a *chakpu*, delicately placed in the palm of his left hand and held by his thumb. This funnel is filled with light blue powder. He holds a similar but empty cone in his right hand and rubs it against the serrated surface of the first funnel. The vibration causes the colored powder to flow out more or less quickly depending on the pressure exerted and the speed with which the right funnel is rubbed against the left. To the western ear this makes a noise like a cricket, but to Tibetans it heralds the approach of emptiness, the sound of higher consciousness.

The cones have openings of various sizes. A thin stream of light blue powder flows out and outlines the perimeter of the small circle in the center of the mandala—the heart of the lotus with eight petals. Then, without encroaching upon this outline, the monk spreads green powder over the heart of the lotus flower. This green soon disappears under new layers, white, then red, followed by blue, and finally yellow, which is actually the only one that will be seen. In this way, the heart of the mandala is made up of a cushion of five colors. The green refers to the lotus, a flower that grows in mud without its beauty being affected, in the same way that Buddha was able to embody spiritual beauty without being hampered by his original defects. White evokes the moon and the pure nature of the *bodhisattvas*, the beings on the path to the Awakening who delay their own achievement and become reincarnated to help others along the path. Red is the fire of knowledge that burns away illusion and ignorance. Blue and yellow are the respective colors of Rahu and Kalagni, two "lunar nodes," according to Tibetan astrology, whose energy helps the achievement of supreme equilibrium.

In a mandala, everything has a meaning; nothing is left to chance.

The monk will set the central Buddha on this cushion. With his funnel filled with an intense blue he draws a *vajra*. This scepter, the emblem of Tibetan Buddhism, symbolizes Kalachakra. To the right of the *vajra* he draws an orange-yellow dot that represents Vishvamata, Kalachakra's consort. The two are inseparable, linked in intimate embrace. Two major Buddhas specific to Tibetans are also present, but invisible, in this lotus center, each one also joined in intimate embrace with his female double: Akshobya and Prajna-paramita, and Vajrasattva and Vajradhatvishvari.

Now all four monks can work together, each in one of the quarters of the diagram, east, south, west, and north. They work from center out towards the periphery, that is, in the opposite direction of that followed by the novice.

The monks have already been initiated, and it is the work that imposes this approach. Eventually the monks can come down from the support and work standing up round the table.

What the novice will see first is that part that the monks have colored in last, the six circles

symbolizing the universe that surround the palace of Kalachakra. He, the novice, is still in the world of phenomena, illusions and passions: he will leave behind anger, jealousy, and lust in the charnel house—the wheels inscribed in the circle of the element "fire."

## "Seed Syllables"

As the novice learns to read, write, think, dream, and imagine, he will discover colors, symbols, a path of development, and also the amazing "seed syllables," written in Sanskrit characters, drawn here and there in the Kalachakra mandala. He will learn that when pronounced correctly, in a low, deep voice, these syllables can create in his mind a deity or an active principle that will help him in his evolution. These Sanskrit characters can also be used as *mantras* or tantric prayers, These syllables have no literal meaning. They are designed to overturn habitual patterns of thought and lead to truths that words cannot express The western initiate John Blofeld explains them as follows: "Skillfully used, *mantras* produce results that range from minor changes in the state of consciousness to overwhelming changes. Used by more advanced followers they can lead to temporary material changes in objects. These are not miracles but an extension of the principle whereby a sustained, even tone can shatter glass."

Once the circles, the charnel houses and the *mantras* have been recognized, there still remain the offerings that must be made to Kalachakra. The gardens filled with offerings are in fact the only areas where the monks constructing a Kalachakra can give free rein to their artistic imagination. In all other parts, the monks have to follow meticulously the instructions codifying a mandala. But this rule does not prevent some "executants" being preferred above others, and subtle nuances can be seen between mandalas. In spite of the strict rules, art has its place.

The novice knows that the Kalachakra Mandala is actually composed of five mandalas, that it is a palace with five levels, although it is made entirely with colored powders, the superimposed layers forming a relief; These five mandalas, three and then two, correspond to each of the levels of this "divine dwelling."

The body, speech, and mind mandalas, with their similar structures, seem to converse with each other. A certain gesture, or *mudra*, of the

Right:
A monk holds his breath;
his concentration is
extreme.

hands and fingers, such as for instance placing the hands on top of each other with the palms upwards, can help in achieving the desired state of consciousness. But, as mentioned earlier, a particular *mantra* and seed syllable, such as the famous Tibetan "om," can do the same. There are pure correspondences between these three levels.

These are followed by the pristine consciousness mandala and the great bliss mandala, the final two levels.

In December 1994 in Barcelona, the Dalai Lama confided that until the age of thirty his understanding of the Kalachakra had been intellectual, but that later on the Kalachakra gradually came to shape his being.[1] He stressed the importance of a compassionate attitude, toward others, a prerequisite for those wanting to progress within this palace. By compassion he meant being available to others, wanting to alleviate their suffering, and helping and respecting all living creatures. Even insects, even a mosquito. "It can bite me once, I wave it away; it comes back, I wave it away again; it comes back yet again, I admit it, I shall kill it in spite of myself! As you see, I am far from being perfect," he once said, smiling.[2]

1. In exile and outside Asia, the Dalai Lama has given the teaching of the Kalachakra on several occaions. In Europe, the first time was at Rikon (Zurich), in 1985. The second was at Bacelona from December 11–18, 1994.

2. See Claude B. Levenson, *Ainsi parle le Dalai Lama*, *Editions Balland, Paris, 1993*.

## Three Inner Channels

Kalachakra is not simply an intellectual exercise. It is not enough to know how to decode a mandala and interpret its symbolism. It is necessary to become abandoned to it and immersed in it, so that it enters the self.

A demanding practice is required, divided into three main stages: "Childhood Initiation," "Generation," and "Accomplishment." When teaching in the west, the Dalai Lama only deals with the "Childhood Initiation" and its seven stages.

The disciple presents himself at the east gate. Guided by a master, he then goes to the north gate of the body mandala, moving clockwise. There he receives the initiation of "Water," comparable to the bathing of a newborn child, followed by the initiation of "Haircutting," the first haircut. Then in front of the south gate of the speech mandala there follows the initiation of the "Crown," like the ear-piercing of a child wearing his first earrings, and that of the "Vajra and the Bell," the child's first words. Having reached the east gate of the mind mandala, the initiation of "Conduct," the apprenticeship of the five senses, and that of the "Name," the naming of the child, take place. The last of these seven initiations, that of "Permission," takes place in front of the west gate of the great bliss mandala and is like a first reading lesson. At this stage, the novice is assumed to have purified his body, his speech, and his mind, so he can now move on from childhood to youth and achieve spiritual maturity.

"Generation" is directed to this maturity and consists of four "higher" stages. The disciple will have to imagine, to "visualize," that is, to conjure up in his mind the 722 deities that correspond to the various states of the Kalachakra

Left:
A monk carries out the dispersal of the mandala in the sea; water is a symbol of impermanence.

on the path to Buddhahood. This requires long sessions of meditation and concentration, based on difficult techniques. But it is only on this condition, having himself followed this long path marked out by these innumerable deities, that the disciple has any hope of approaching the center and identifying with Kalachakra in intimate union with his female consort.

The disciple is constantly reminded of the correspondences between the external and internal Kalachakras. "External" is a concept that in this palace refers to the astral world, the external environment and its forces. "Internal" refers to the laws of the body with its breathing and its energies.

According to Tibetan anatomy, three channels run through the human body from the bottom to the top. The left channel, *kyangma*, is male, white, containing the seminal fluid, and is influenced by the moon. The right channel, *roma*, is female, red, filled with blood, and is influenced by the sun. The disciple has to learn to bring together these two channels in the central channel, *Ooma*, which is blue and influenced by the two lunar nodes, Rahu and Kalagni. The "Alternate Kalachakra" is the practice of this union in which the internal and external Kalachakras communicate and merge. Uniting the male and female components, the white and red, the lunar and solar, the seminal fluid and blood, is to merge with Kalachakra embracing Vishvamata, because Kalachakra is linked to the Moon and Vishvamata to the Sun. At this point the disciple is on the threshold of the "Accomplishment" and the last four stages, known as the "higher of the higher."

Six very complex yogas[3] that stimulate sexual energy will help the disciple to cross these final levels: the "yoga of retreat", the "yoga of stabilization", the "yoga of breath control," the "yoga of retention," the "yoga of attention," and finally the "yoga of samadhi". The tantric practitioner dissolves his energies in the central canal, bringing together the blood and seminal fluid. For his retention work he may be calling upon a real female partner or work from a mental image, imagining or "visualizing" himself bonding with his consort. He is expected to leave his mortal shell, cut himself off from the cycle of becoming, and achieve the pure essence, blending together the 21,600 male "blisses" with the 21,600 female "blisses." Finally the four faces of Kalachakra are reached: the black, to the east, wrathful; the red, to the south, exalted; the yellow, to the west, at peace; the white, to the north, fulfilled; all are now his.

3. Yoga is a rigorous practice of physical and mental discipline that makes possible the achievement of the union of the individual and the "Divine Source."

The cosmos according to Kalachakra. *Thangka*,
Völkerkundemuseum (ethnographical museum),
University of Zurich.

# External Mandala, Internal Mandala

Martin Brauen

In contrast to the medieval cosmology in Europe, Buddhist teaching does not consider either the earth or man to be the center of the universe. Buddhism holds that there are principal gods, and secondary deities residing in their immediate environment—beings with an ethereal body or purely formless beings— who constitute the theocentric core of the universe, while human beings, or any other living creature, exist outside this core, subject to time.

In tantric "visualization" exercises, and especially in the very complex ritual of the mandala, the disciple must try (once more) to reach this core inhabited by deities. The mandala is the mirror of the cosmos, not only in its external form. It is also the mirror of another microcosm: man. The mandala is based on the assumption of a very close relationship between the universe, the mandalic circle, and human beings.

Besides the importance given to the Divinity, Buddhist cosmology is notable for the multiplication of microcosms producing the formation of a conglomerate of countless "cosmic clusters" (see illustration 1). This is very close to the vision that Western science has of the universe today. Thousands of cosmic systems of this kind, each including a Mount Meru, a Sun and a Moon, planets, worlds inhabited by deities, etc., make up a small cosmos. Thousands of small cosmoses

Illustration 1
The starting point of this reconstruction of a "cosmic cluster" is that all cosmic systems rest on the same surface in space. Buddhist texts give no information concerning the possible existence of other "cosmic clusters" that are situated beyond or below the surface illustrated here.

constitute a medium cosmos and thousands of medium cosmoses constitute a *"gigantus"* cosmos that is made up of thousands of millions of other cosmic systems.

The periods during which these systems, doomed to disappear according to Tantric Buddhism, are formed may also be described as gigantic. They contain a "waiting space" that will finally be set in motion again by a wind that arrives without making a sound. This will encourage the establishment of a new system of worlds. In the same way that humans are transitory, so the world and universe also undergo constant change.

# The Pyramidal Cosmos according to Kalachakra Tradition

Buddhism recognizes several cosmogonies without becoming tangled up in contradictions. Indeed, according to Kalu Rinpoche, "Any one of these various cosmologies is completely valid for the beings whose karmic projections cause them to experience their universe in that way. There is a certain relativity in the way one experiences the world. This means that all the possible experiences of every being in the six realms of existence ... arc based upon karmic inclinations and degrees of individual development. Thus, on a relative level any cosmology is valid. On an ultimate level, no cosmology is absolutely true.

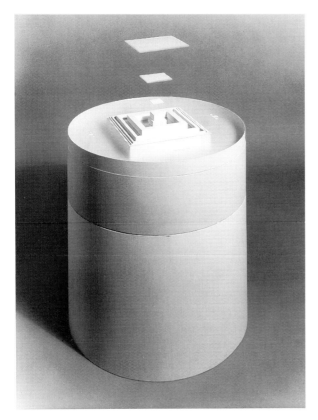

Illustration 2
Scale representation of a cosmos according to the concept of Abhidharmakosha. The upper part of the cylinder (the salt seas and the fresh water seas) has an area of 80,000 *yojanas*; according to Abhidharmakosha tradition, a *yojana* is 9.32 miles (15 km) long, while according to Kalachakra tradition, a *yojana* is equivalent to 4.66 miles (7.5 km).

WEST

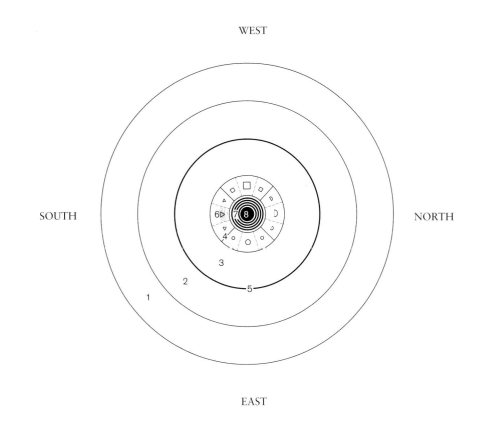

SOUTH

NORTH

EAST

Illustration 3
The cosmos according to
Kalachakra, seen from above

1. the disc of air
2. the disc of fire
3. the disc of water
4. the disc of earth
5. the mountain of fire
6. the south continent
   (Jambudvipa) with seven
   mountain chains
7. six rock faces and six oceans
8. the base of Mount Meru

It cannot be universally valid, given the different conventional situations of beings."[1]

In Tibetan Buddhism there are two main concepts of the cosmos, that of Abhidharmakosha (see ill. 2) and that of Kalachakra (see ills. 3 to 6). But the tradition that is recorded in the *Kalachakra Tantra* has rarely been described in Western publications as a philosophy that is independent of, and very different from, the Abhidharmakosha tradition.

As in the Abhidharmakosha philosophy, the Kalachakra system starts from the principle that the different cosmoses appear after immeasurable lengths of time to disappear and be reborn again. However, in contrast to the Abhidharmakosha concept, the Kalachakra

tradition does not assert that the five elements totally disappear at the end of each period. According to Kalachakra, the elements break up and atoms of space keep them apart from each other. Due to the stockpile of "collective *karma*," accumulated in the past, the atoms form new combinations between themselves. The atoms of the air come together, causing violent winds whose effect is to bring together the atoms of fire. This in turn triggers off lightning, that is, electricity. This is followed by the formation of water atoms, which leads to rain. The rainbows are the first manifestations of the atoms of the earth. They become increasingly dense until they finally become solid earth. The atoms of space fill the gaps between the other atoms and thus float above and below the system of cosmic worlds formed in this way.

These two theories of cosmogony have one thing in common, that is, the concept of a concentric construction of the universe, in the style of a mandala, with a Mount Meru in the center. The shape of this mountain differs in

1. Kalu Rinpoche, 1990.

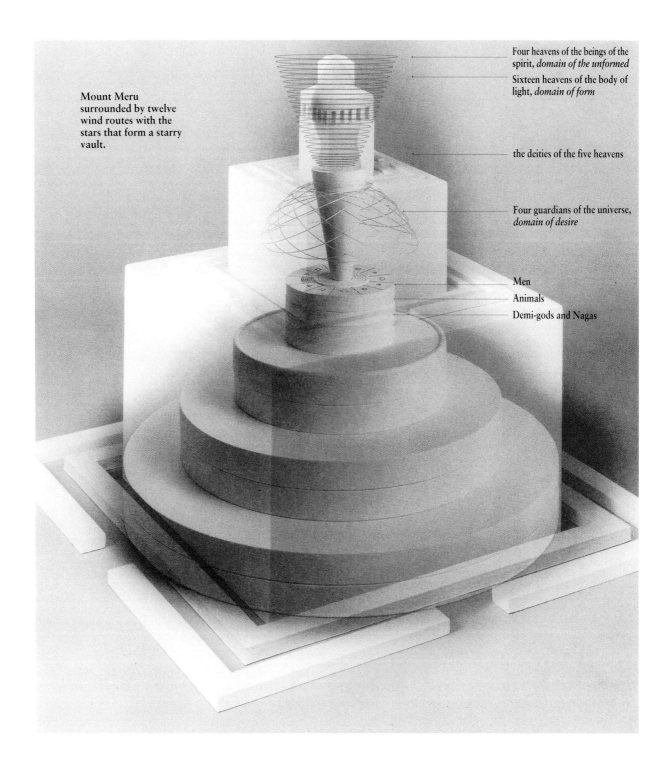

Mount Meru surrounded by twelve wind routes with the stars that form a starry vault.

Four heavens of the beings of the spirit, *domain of the unformed*

Sixteen heavens of the body of light, *domain of form*

the deities of the five heavens

Four guardians of the universe, *domain of desire*

Men

Animals

Demi-gods and Nagas

Illustration 4
*Representation of the cosmos according to Kalachakra with the palace of the Kalachakra Mandala in the background:*
The Kalachakra system, like the Abhidharmakosha system, has twelve continents—three for each of the four directions—floating in the middle of a large ocean surrounding Mount Meru. The southern continent, divided into six domains, is called Jambudvipa and provides a home for animals and men. The continents are represented in the form of rectangles, circles, etc.
The superimposition of the two images also shows the correlation between the cosmos according to Kalachakra and the palace of Kalachakra as described in the text and detailed further in illustration 9.

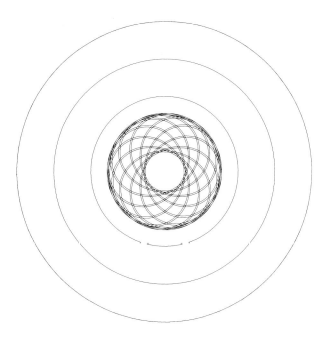

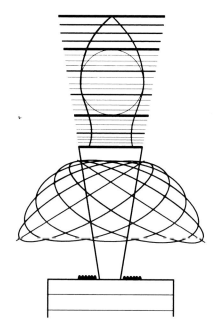

Illustration 5

Illustration 6

the two systems. The foundation of the Kalachakra cosmos is different from that of the Abhidharmakosha cosmos. It is made up of four giant discs, the lower disc (the air disc) having the largest diameter (400,000 yojanas, 4 million miles or 6 million kilometres), and the top disc having the smallest diameter (100,000 yojanas, 1 million miles or 1.5 million kilometres). Mount Meru has no angles, unlike that of Abhidharmakosha; it is round (see ills. 3 and 4).

Mount Meru is surrounded by six rock faces. This model of the world shows the twelve routes or circles of winds round Mount Meru. The planets appear to float on these circles of wind, orbiting around Mount Meru.[2] Pictorial representations of these twelve wind routes can be found in the monasteries of

Bhutan (cf. ill. 5). They show the routes seen from above, from a point situated just above the cosmos. Admittedly such representations do not show the layout of the routes in space. Only a side view, created by a three-dimensional computer program imitating the cosmos, reveals that these orbits form a kind of cupola opening up around the Meru mountain.

What is noticeable about the Kalachakra concept of the world is that the universe beyond Mount Meru looks like a head invisible to our human eyes. A head with a neck, a chin, a nose, a forehead, and a protuberance above the head in the shape of hair tied together in a topknot (see ill. 4, *Representation of the Cosmos according to Kalachakra*).

This invisible head in human form contains twenty-four of the heavens of the Kalachakra universe: a way of expressing that there is a particular relationship between the human and divine forms.

This reveals the wisdom of the Kalachakra tradition: the infinite repetition of structures constantly oscillating between the macrocosm and microcosm, and vice-versa.

2. The function of the twelve wind routes is not entirely clear. According to one conception, the twelve wind routes will only carry the Sun (Imaeda, 1987, p. 630, and oral opinions of A. Berzin). The circles are apparently also related to the twenty-seven lunar houses (Nakshatra).

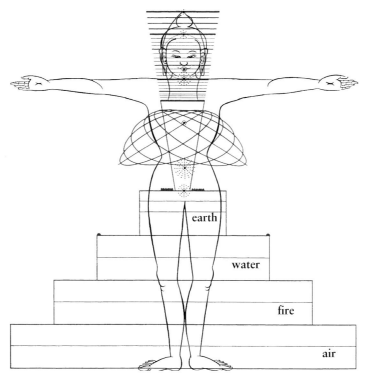

Illustration 7
Structural correlations between the Kalachakra universe and the human body.

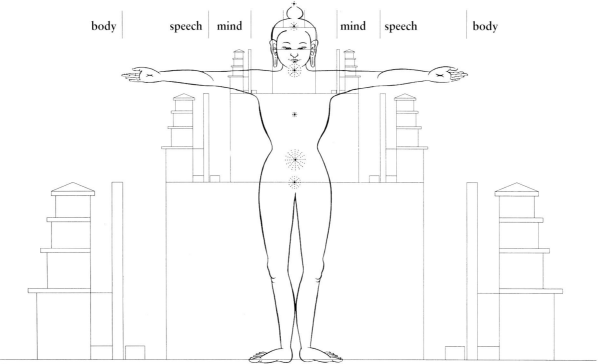

Illustration 8
Structural correlations between the palace of the Kalachakra Mandala and the human body.

# Analogy between Man and the Cosmos

The theory of structural relationships between things and their interaction, between the universe, the mandala and the human body, undergoes a complex process of development in the *Kalachakra Tantra*.

The *Kalachakra Tantra*, or "Tantra of the Wheel of Time," speaks of three closely interwoven levels: the external level, the internal level, and the alternative level or "other" wheel of time. The external wheel of time is made up of all the external manifestations of the human environment, that is, the universe with its discs of elements, Mount Meru, and the winds. The internal Kalachakra is made up of those who live in this environment: human beings. Their structure, construction, and inner periodicity correspond very precisely to the external wheel of time. Finally, the alternative Kalachakra is the teaching of these

analogies and correlations including the practices resulting from it: yoga, a form of "mental judo" (to quote the words of A. Berzin) that teaches one to use the powers of the internal and external wheels of time, instead of oppose them.

The external Kalachakra and internal Kalachakra have many points of similarity (see ill. 7). The shape of the head visible in the upper part of the cosmos according to Kalachakra looks amazingly like a human head. The greatest horizontal extent of the universe corresponds to its maximum height, in the same way that in human beings the distance from finger tip to finger tip with outstretched arms corresponds to the total height of the body (4 cubits). The four superimposed circles of elements make up half the altitude of the universe, in the same way that in a

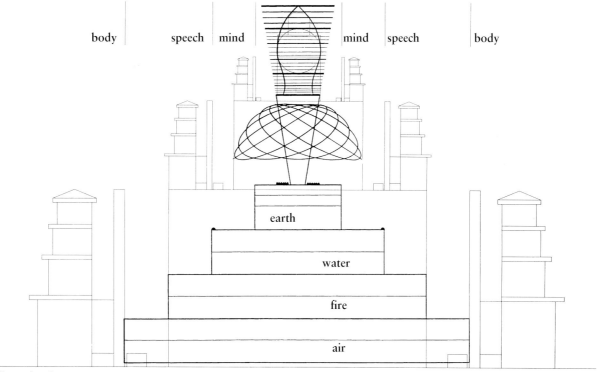

Illustration 9
Structural correlations between the cosmos according to Kalachakra and the palace of the Kalachakra Mandala.

human being the distance between the feet and the pelvic bones is half the overall height.

By projecting the image of a man on a representation of the Kalachakra universe, it is obvious that Mount Meru is superimposed on the human spine, a correspondence that Tucci observed.[3] As regards the routes of the winds, the orbits of the stars and planets, they correspond to the breaths that circulate in the human body and that, according to Tantrism and the mandala ritual, must be purified and controlled.[4]

There are other correlations between the human body and the Kalachakra mandala. When the image of a man is projected on the graphic representation of a palace, in other words the central part of a Kalachakra mandala (see ill. 8), the lower part of the palace, the body mandala, corresponds to the legs; the middle part (the speech mandala) to the chest (especially to the lungs and thorax); and the mind mandala to the head. In addition, it is clearly apparent that the distance between the two shoulders correlates with the sphere of the mind; the distance between the elbows correlates with the sphere of the speech; and the distance between right-hand fingertips and the left-hand fingertips correlates with the sphere

of the body. It is particularly important to stress that the point between the two eyebrows, which plays a vital part in the meditation exercises reserved for higher levels of yoga, coincides exactly with the center of the mind mandala. Here reside the highest mandalic deities: Kalachakra and Vishvamata.

Other analogies become apparent when the image of the universe and that of the palace of the mandala are superimposed on one another(see ill. 9). The four discs of the elements (the fifth element, ether, does not appear because it has no vertical extension) correspond to the body mandala. Mount Meru, the winds that blow round it, and the planets correspond to the mandala.

The height of the palace and the width of the base of the palace are identical (32 arm lengths, about 200 feet or 60 metres each), as are the height and width of the cosmos.

The same is true of the lower disc of the cosmos (air) and the body mandala, the fire disc and the base of the body mandala, the water disc and the speech mandala, while the earth disc corresponds to the mind mandala. Finally, the upper diameter of Mount Meru corresponds to the internal width of the mind mandala.

# Man as Mandala

In the Kalachakra tradition, the universe and the human body match up perfectly, not only externally in their composition but also on other levels. The palace in the mandala is made up of several levels: the levels of body, speech, and mind. This last level is itself further divided into two. This structure is also that of man, a fact we shall return to later.

**The Body**
For Buddhists the body of each individual consists of five transitory aggregates that themselves are combined with each other (*skandha*). They are the aggregate of form, the aggregate of sensations, the aggregate of perceptions, the aggregate of mental formations, and the aggregate of consciousness. In the Kalachakra tradition there is an additional *skandha*: the aggregate of wisdom. In addition, the

---

3. Tucci, *op. cit.*, 1989, p. 105
4. An exact correspondence between the winds on which the planets are riding and the main breaths in the human being is not easy to detect. Generally, it is a question of the ten vital essential breaths in the human being, but in a conference at Madison, Serkong Rinpoche spoke of twelve human breaths. It is the same for the planets—Sun, Moon, Mercury, Venus, Mars, Jupiter, Saturn—and the two lunar nodes: Rahu (north node), Kalagni (south node) and the comet Encke.

constituents of man also include the five elements: ether, air, fire, water, earth, and sometimes a sixth element, infinite knowledge. Like the elements, the aggregates belong to the level of the body. In the Kalachakra mandala and in the mandala initiations linked to this tradition, the aggregates and the elements, represented by symbols and directed towards the four cardinal points, reveal that the human body can be considered a mandala in its own right.

## Speech

According to the tantric concept, 72,000 invisible channels (*nadi*, *rtsa*) and energy-laden winds (*prana* or *vayu*) run through the human body. The winds and channels, laden with energy, are among the most important components of the human body on the speech level. Two of the three main channels are situated on the right and left of the spine, and the third channel, the middle one, is slightly in front of the spine. The central channel (*dbu ma*[5]) passes through the genitals and the centre of the body up to the top of the head, where it bends slightly to the front to end finally between the eyes. The left channel or white channel (*rkyang ma*[6]) runs from the left nostril to a finger's width from the lower end of the central channel, while the right channel or red channel (*ro ma*[7]) starts from the right nostril and runs down the body. The left channel is linked with the moon and the right channel with the sun.

At certain points along the central *nadi* are the six *chakras*,[8] also known as "lotus flowers" (*Padma*). According to the Kalachakra tradition, each of these energy centers is situated at the same level respectively as the sexual organs,[9] the navel, the heart, the throat, the forehead, and the top of the head. The *chakras* are generally represented by lotus flowers (see ill. 10). The number of petals on the flower depends on the energy channels that flow into the corresponding *chakra*.

The wind channel on the left turns round the central channel, clockwise and level with the *chakras*. The wind channel on the right

---

5. *Chandali, Avadhuti, Sushumna* (Sanskrit)

6. *Lalana* or *Ida* (Sanskrit).
7. *Rasana* or *Pingala* (Sanskrit).
8. In India, the word *chakra* has several meanings: wheel, disc, potter's wheel, and circle. The Kalachakra tradition typically speaks of six chakras; in India the number usually given is seven.
9. Often people speak of the *chakra* in the "secret region," while in this article, it is referred to as the "sexual chakra."

*Crown Chakra*: wheel of supreme happiness — lotus with 4 petals

*Forehead Chakra*: wheel of wind — lotus with 16 petals

*Throat Chakra*: wheel of enjoyment — lotus with 32 petals

*Heart Chakra*: wheel of phenomena — lotus with 8 petals

*Navel Chakra*: wheel of creation — lotus with 64 petals

*Sexual Chakra*:[9] wheel of conservation of happiness — lotus with 32 petals

Illustration 10

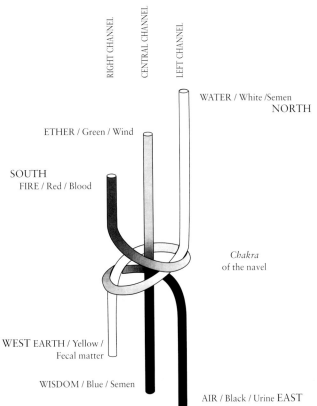

RIGHT CHANNEL   CENTRAL CHANNEL   LEFT CHANNEL

WATER / White /Semen
NORTH

ETHER / Green / Wind

SOUTH
FIRE / Red / Blood

*Chakra*
of the navel

WEST EARTH / Yellow /
Fecal matter

WISDOM / Blue / Semen

AIR / Black / Urine EAST

**Illustration 11**
Attempt at a graphic representation of the three main channels situated above or below the *navel chakra*. Water, ether, and air are seen as the male side; fire, earth, and wisdom are seen as the female side.

functions in the same way, but counter-clockwise. According to the Kalachakra tradition, this seriously hampers the free circulation of wind but does not prevent it completely. Reading the descriptions left by the first Dalai Lama, Gen Dun Drup,[10] the three main channels seem to form a mandala between themselves and are divided into two parts: an upper part, rising from the navel to the top of the head, and a lower part, descending from the navel down to the sexual organs or the anus. Using the colors named and recommended by the first Dalai Lama, one obtains a picture that shows that in Tantric Buddhism even the human body and its various parts are considered mandalas.

The winds pulsating in the channels transport the components of consciousness and enable all the activities of the body and mind to take place, which would be impossible without them. "The downward emptying wind" controls the movements of the white and red *bodhicitta*[11] (male and female drops), urine, and excrement. "The fire-accompanying wind" separates the energy-providing components in food from the useless ones and kindles the inner fire (*gtum mo*). "The life-holding wind" oversees the smooth operation of the breathing in and out through the nose.[12]

In Tantric Buddhism, the winds or breaths are considered causes of cyclic existence, but they also contain the seeds of Enlightenment. It is for this reason that the yoga of the mandala ritual insists on the importance of the winds, their purification, and their positive use in order to reach Enlightenment.

10. Mullin, 1986.

11. Here the word *bodhicitta* does not refer to desire for enlightenment; it means "drop" (*bindu; thigle*). Every human being contains white *bodhicitta* drops (male) or red drops (female).
12. Lati Rinpoche / Hopkins, 1990, and Dhargyey, 1985.

| EXTERNAL KALACHAKRA | INTERNAL KALACHAKRA |
|---|---|
| 1 year = 12 months | 1 day = 12 shifts of breath |
| 1 month = 30 days of 60 units (i.e. 1,800 units) | 1 shift of breath- 1,800 breaths |
| 1 year = 21,600 (12 x 1,800) units of time | 1 day = 21,600 (12 x 1,800) breaths |

Table 1
Correspondence between the external Kalachakra (cosmos)
and the internal wheel of time (man) in relation to units of time

According to the Kalachakra system, the human being contains ten essential winds[13] that are in correlation with the elements and cardinal points,[14] thereby forming a mandala in the body.

The correspondences between the external world (universe) and internal world (man) go much further: the twelve respiratory cycles carried out in twenty-four hours of human life correspond to the twelve months of the year. In the same way that there are months in which the days "increase," that is become longer, and months in which days "decrease," there are, according to the tantric concept, identical changes of rhythm in the respiratory movements in the course of a single day. In one half of the day, breathing takes place mainly through the right nostril, then during the second half of the day, mainly through the left one. In this way the breath sometimes flows through the right channel—that is, the one which is related to the Sun—and sometimes through the channel on the left, which is assigned to the Moon.

In one "shift of the breath," man takes 1,800 breaths, known as karmic (inner) winds. Thus, he breathes in and out 21,600 times (12 x 1,800) a day. Each of the twelve groups of 1,800 breaths must be purified during the stages known as "Accomplishment," in other words the last four stages of the practice of the Kalachakra mandala.

Winds determine internal as well as external processes. While external winds are produced by the collective *karma*, internal breaths are produced by the individual *karma*. The ten main winds that circulate through the twenty-seven constellations in the right channel or left channel correspond in the external Kalachakra to the winds that blow round Mount Meru, where the ten planets cross the twenty-seven constellations of the zodiacs of the north and south.

13. Five of these winds correspond to the five main winds in the other tantric systems: however, the five other winds of the Kalachakra system are not identical to the five secondary winds of other schools. Connections between the human body and the winds are also found in Hinduism. So, in the *Chandogya Upanishad*, one speaks of five winds having correlations with the five cardinal points, the five channels, the five senses, the deities and the five elements (sun, moon, fire, water, wind). After Mus, 1933, II, pp. 441–450.
14. According to Dhargyey, 1985, p. 119, as well as Tenzin Gyatso, 1985.

## The Mind

According to Tantric Buddhism, man is not only endowed with a body and speech; he also has other faculties, that of the mind: six senses as well as six objects of senses, six faculties for different actions and six actions that on the basis of symbols attached to them can in turn form a mandala. In addition, there is also a fourth domain of the mind, a super-mind: it is that of the "great bliss" and "deep awareness," and is represented by a bell in connection with the center of the mandala (see table 2).

| BODY | | SPEECH | | MIND | | |
|---|---|---|---|---|---|---|
| Six elements | Six aggregates | Ten winds | Channels | Six senses | Six faculties of action | Emblems / direction |
| Air | Aggregate of mental formations | Fire-accompanying wind[1] and tortoise wind[2] | Bottom left | Smell | Faculty of the mouth | Sword / East |
| Fire | Aggregate of sensations | Upward-moving wind[3] and lizard wind[4] | Top right | Sight | Faculty of the arms | Jewel / South |
| Water | Aggregate of perceptions | Pervading wind[5] and devadatta[6] | Top left | Taste | Faculty of the leg | Lotus / North |
| Earth | Aggregate of form | Serpent wind[7] and Dhanamjaya wind[8] | Bottom right | Touch | Faculty of defecation | Wheel / West |
| Ether | Aggregate of consciousness | Life-holding wind[9] | Top center | Hearing | Faculty of urination | Vajra / top |
| Supreme happiness | Pristine consciousness | Downward-emptying wind[10] | Bottom center | Spirit | Faculty of ejaculation | Bell / bottom |
| Six female buddhas | Six male buddhas | Ten *shaktis* | Kalachakra and Vishvamata | Six *bodhisattvas* | Six wrathful deities | |

Table 2

This text is extracted from *Das Mandala—Der Heilige Kreis im Tantrishen Buddhismus*, DuMont, Cologne, 1992.

Left:
The Shakyamuni Buddha,
fourteenth century,
monastery of Pelkor Chode
Monastery, Gyantse
(central Tibet).

# History and Legend

Claude B. Levenson

Made from sand, metal or stone, conceived by the gods and crafted by man, developed grain by grain, painted or embroidered on fabric, made from material chosen as if to emphasize its impermanence, the mandala with its universal resonances is inseparable from Buddhism, particularly Tibetan Buddhism. Far away, high up on the roof of the world in the heart of the Himalayas, in one of the many chapels of the vast red and white Potala Palace, which dominates the secular capital of Tibet with its subtle balance of power and serenity, there is an extremely precious three-dimensional mandala.

It is the dwelling of a formidable deity, the Black Lord of transcendental wisdom, the Master of Time, and at the same time the materialization of his kingdom of the Pure Land. This masterpiece of Tibetan religious art was produced in the seventeenth century. It was commissioned by Sangye Gyatso, the regent who ruled the country after the long-concealed death of the fifth Dalai Lama.

A visitor today can still marvel at the sight of the effigies of the 172 lamas entrusted with the transmission of the teachings of the Kalachakra. Or they can linger before the statues of the seven religious kings and the twenty-five *kalkis* or "spiritual guides" of the mythical kingdom of Shambala. There are thirty-eight deities, who have a part to play in this distinguished *tantra*. Among them are Manjusri, the *bodhisattva* of Wisdom, riding a lion, Palden Lhamo, the deity protecting the Dalai Lamas and Lhasa, and Guru Rinpoche, the Precious Master. All keep watch over a place that is imbued with an enduring mysticism.

Elsewhere, in the imposing silence of the infinite Himalayan solitude, a mandala, in this case a natural one, continues to attract travelers, ascetics, pilgrims, and those looking for the absolute, as it has done throughout the centuries. They travel on the rough paths of a pilgrimage to the outer limits of devotion and the sacred. In these plains, Kailash, "like a vast temple whose columns are the mountains, whose vault is the sky and whose altar is the earth" (Giuseppe Tucci), plays the part of Mount Meru or "axis of the world" and "Jewel of the Snows" for the Tibetans who worship it as "Kang Rinpoche." For Hindus it is also the domain of Shiva, the Great Ascetic, whose influence is to be found as well in the original text of the Kalachakra or Wheel of Time, brought back from Shambala by intrepid adventurers of the spirit.

The long history of the Kalachakra Mandala, often inseparable from legend, and its transmission through time and throughout the world goes back to the Sage of the Sakya clan, the historic Buddha, who taught it in the sixth century BC.

According to tradition, the Buddha himself was the first to describe the mandala and expound the complex teachings associated with it. Some say that it was in the twilight years of his life on earth, while others declare that it was shortly after attaining Enlightenment, that he passed on these teachings to a select circle of disciples, including the great king of Shambala, Suchandra, also a member of the Sakya clan, who had requested it. The authentic tantric tradition is not accessible to everyone; it demands profound knowledge and only a very small number of followers are capable of grasping its essence. It is also said that shortly before entering the serene peace of the last accomplishment, the Enlightened One took on the appearance of the powerful deity, Kalachakra, in a body of light perceptible only to the eye of knowledge, revealing the path of ultimate liberation to the wise men and gods who had gathered to witness this event near the *stupa* (or reliquary) of Dhanyakataka in southern India, not far from Madras. At the same time, the Buddha was also at Vultures' Peak Mountain, near Bodhgaya, in northern India, where he appeared in another form and taught the Book of the Perfection of Wisdom, the *Prajnaparamita Sutra*.

Contained in the holy texts of the Kanjur and forming the basis of the Tibetan canon, these mystic teachings have been communicated in a spiritual dimension imperceptible to the ordinary eye but one that is nevertheless as real as ours. Suchandra, King of Shambala, the land of Shiva, returned to his distant kingdom with this invaluable knowledge and immediately recorded it onto tablets—12,000 verses, according to tradition. In addition, he built a three-dimensional mandala close to the capital of his kingdom, at the heart of a grove of sandalwood trees. It was made of five precious stones: gold, silver, turquoise, coral, and pearls, to facilitate the visualization required for meditation. Not content with having produced the first commentaries, he initiated all the subjects of his 96 feudal dis-

tricts into this wisdom. Through the dust of centuries, a veil of peace and oblivion fell upon the happy kingdom devoted to study and the practice of this knowledge, under the leadership of a long line of religious monarchs, each of whom reigned for almost a hundred years.

No one will be astonished at the intertwining of history and legend in the text of the *Anuttarayoga Tantra*, which is in the "mother" category, the supreme level of traditional teaching. Shambala is to Tibet what the Sacred Mountain is to others, the very heart of the world, the passage from the visible to the invisible, even the future Golden Age. A symbol of the point at which infinity and eternity intersect, this magical land exists through the power of the knowledge of which it is the repository: invested with the humblest beliefs coupled with the most audacious speculations transmitted through the centuries by the exploits of the founding heroes, it has constantly been enriched by the perceptions of generations of meditating disciples, ascetics, and travelers on the journey towards knowledge and accomplishment, and the perception of the great wise men. To get to Shambala, one only need follow the guide, while bearing in mind that not only the unwary but serious searchers have lost their way en route to the absolute. Even in the land of awakened dreams, shimmering mirages can conceal real dangers.

Mount Kailash, in Tibet, is seen as the axis of the world. The plain that gives access to this natural mandala is enlivened by scarves of happiness, left as offerings by the pilgrims.

The history of Shambala itself translates and sums up the paradox of the quest. Closely linked to the Wheel of Time, it is one of the most secret initiations because it is extremely complex to master and requires a vast knowledge of the most varied aspects of the tradition. And yet it is the only initiation of the *Anuttarayoga Tantra* that takes place openly, at least in the early stages, before as diverse an audience as possible: anyone who shows the slightest interest can take part. Mere presence at such a ceremony is deemed beneficial, since it is believed to bring about a rebirth in the secret kingdom, that is considered to be the guardian of the purity of the teaching and guarantor of the permanence of the Good Law.

# The Wise Men of the Himalayas

Is this strange kingdom whose name means "source of happiness" a myth or reality? "The answer is not straightforward," the Dalai Lama explained to me one day. Looking at a map of the world, it is quite difficult to identify the precise location of this fabulous land. It is said in the guide books that passing through Bodhgaya, traveling north towards the Himalayas, you eventually arrive at a formidable rampart of snow and ice... "We, Buddhists, believe that there is indeed such a place as heaven or paradise, or rather a Pure Land, close to our everyday universe. But ordinary man cannot see it or go there. No one, in fact, can reach it without following particular practices, through meditation or perhaps through dreaming. Moreover, it is important that the intentions of those who venture along this path should be pure, devoid of selfishness and malicious intent. Otherwise it is impossible to reach Shambala, because it is a very different world from ours. And yet it is not simply a spiritual vision; on the contrary, it exists materially in our universe. If so many fundamental teachings have reached us from Shambala, how could it be just a legend?"

When the teaching is perfectly understandable and follows without any deviation the meticulous subtleties of the sand mandala, when real geography masks a parallel reality while revealing it, the path of the quest brings echoes of El Dorado or the Holy Grail: the road is initiatory and ends with questions where time joins space, questions to which everyone is obliged to provide his own answer. This answer requires the impeccability of the warrior who is prepared to face any challenge, or the inner vision that enables the poet to perceive that which the simple mortal has forgotten, if indeed he ever knew it. They are only words, but it is with them that man builds the walls that imprison him and it is perhaps when waking from this kind of collective hallucination that he is able to recognize the power of his own mind.

This at least is what the wise men of the Himalayas say, and it is a way of approaching this famous Wheel of Time, without which there is no fabulous land, no irresistible urge to set out, and no thirst for knowledge to reach it. According to the Buddhist vision we must learn to be free so that we can be released from all our chains—be they gold or iron—and achieve the primordial unity of the three kingdoms, physical, mental and spiritual. This is the teaching of the Kalachakra.

Myth or reality, myths and truths... Century after century, the wise men of the Tibetan mountains followed ther predecessors in their quest for Shambala. Sometimes they found it. In the process they succeeded in handing down a great dream that sometimes appears like history and sometimes like prophecy.

This is because Suchandra, the blessed king of Shambala, who was himself the incarnation of a saint and who was the first to benefit from the teachings of Shakyamuni, incarnated in a Kalachakra's body, eventually disappeared, leaving other enlightened monarchs to reign over Shambala and ensure the transmission of this sacred teaching. However, in about the first century AD the monarch Yashas, the eighth ruler in the line and considered to be an emanation of Manjusri, the *boddhisattva* of Wisdom, agreed to produce what might be called an abridged version of the Kalachakra at the urgent request of his subjects. This text would form the basis of subsequent teachings and is still given today by great masters authorized to reveal the Kalachakra, including the present Dalai Lama.

## Towards the Year 2400

Dating from this period there is a second line of twenty-five sovereigns, known as kalkis. This line still exists and from it one day, soon perhaps, or in about the year 2400 as forecast by the prophecy, will come the King-Propagator (the twenty-fifth *kalki*) who will overcome adversity and defeat the forces of evil. Throughout this period, in the world outside of Shambala, that is to say on earth, events have continued to take their course. From the seventh and eighth centuries onwards, in the land where once the Bon religion ruled, Buddhism began to follow a mystical path. In time, the history of the precious teachings came to the ears of an ascetic, Chilupa, a great Indian yogi of the eleventh century. He decided to go and search for this forgotten knowledge and set out on the way to Shambala.

And yet, the famous sage failed to reach the heart of the lotus that forms the legendary land governed by its omniscient king. Far from the world of men, at the top of a very high mountain, he met a hermit who asked him why he had undertaken this hazardous journey. He warned Chilupa that the way to Shambala was long, and that he would face many dangers on the road to the bastion of knowledge, that the way was carefully guarded by the snow leopard, clouds, and mist. Nevertheless, he offered to introduce his passing guest there and then to the knowledge that he was seeking. Then the pilgrim recognized Manjusri, the *bodhisattva* of Wisdom, prostrated himself before him, and was introduced to the mysteries of the Kalachakra. On his return, Chilupa's enthusiasm for the teaching was such that he was given the name Kalachakrapada, "Kalachakra the Elder," and having won a famous philosophical debate with the abbot of the great Buddhist university of Nalanda, the celebrated sage Naropa, he personally initiated him into this meditative practice.

It is believed that the lost teachings returned to India in this way.

But according to another version (there are several version of the return of Kalachakra to its origins) it was Shripala himself, the seventh *kalki* of Shambala, who in 1027 brought the teachings of the Kalachakra back to India.

However that may be, there is one fact that can be confirmed by history: at the beginning of the eleventh century AD, the Kalachakra was known in India. The basic texts that circulated in Sanskrit are dated 1012.

At about the same time this influential doctrine was flourishing in Kashmir and Bengal. From there it spread through the vast Himalayan mountain range. From Bengal the precious heritage was transmitted by Naropa to Atisha, and from Kashmir by the master Somanatha. Both became experts in the new teachings and passed on their knowledge to the monks of the high plateau.

## Four Volumes of Commentaries

The oldest known commentary is dated 1026. It is the work of the translator Dro who entitled it "The Great Commentary of the Tantra of Kalachakra, the Immaculate Light." Gradually this wisdom became one of the pillars of Tibetan Buddhism, with minute variations depending on schools and eras. The other, no less important, tradition dates from the twelfth century and is called Rwa after the Tibetan translator Rwa Lotsawa, a pupil of the great Kashmiri sage Somanatha. This version reached its peak with the great scholars Bu-don (1290–1364) and Dolba-ba (1292–1361), of the School of the Ancient Ones, the Nyingma, also known as the Red Hats. It was to a master of this line of scholars that Tsong Khapa (1357–1419) was apprenticed, having received his first initiation from a direct disciple of Bu-don.

Tsong Khapa, the great Tibetan scholar and reformer, founder of the school of Gelugpa, became particularly interested in this technique of meditation, into which he was subsequently personally and completely initiated by the sovereign of the forbidden kingdom. From scholar to ascetic, from hermit to sage, from master to disciple, the line of transmission has continued without interruption throughout the centuries. Kedrup Gelek Belsang (1385–1438), himself a close disciple of Tsong Khapa, wrote four volumes of commentaries on the Kalachakra that became with time one of the fundamental texts of the Gelugpa, "those who advocate virtue," also known as the Yellow Hats, which is the order of the Dalai Lama. Several texts, more or less long, more or less obscure, came into existence, completing each other and clarifying several aspects of the quest according to the understanding of each author. There are even guide books to help those in search of the mysterious land of Shambala, the most famous one being written by the third Panchen Lama, Lobsang Palden Yeshe, *The Way to Shambala*, which dates from 1775.

For the present Dalai Lama, "The initiation of the Kalachakra is one of the most important in Buddhism because this *tantra* takes everything into account: the human body and mind, the whole external aspect, cosmic and astrological. By its complete practice, it is possible to achieve Awakening in a single life. We believe firmly in its power to reduce conflicts, we believe it is capable of creating peace, peace of mind, and consequently of encouraging

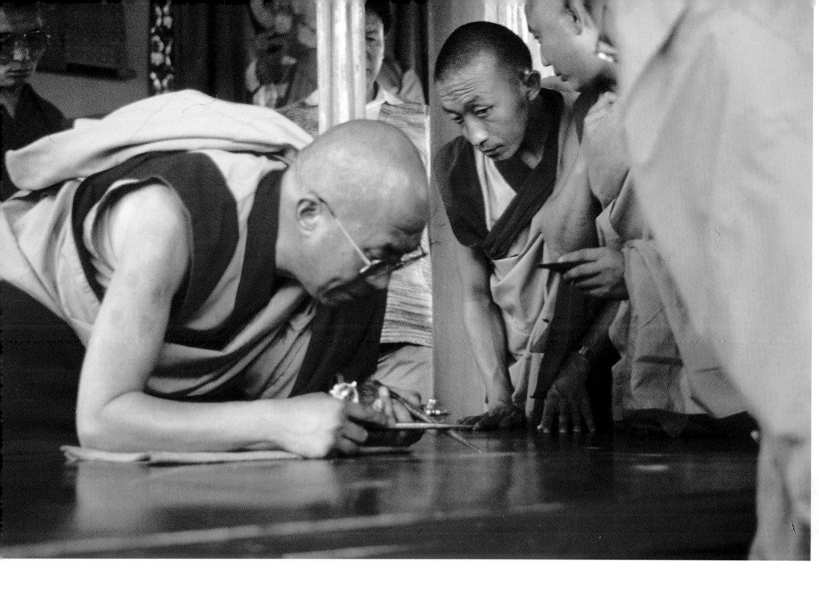

peace in the world. One day, in the centuries to come, the kingdom of Sham-bala might very well reappear in the reality that appears to be ours, and thus contribute to the task that is still to be accomplished in this world." Learned lamas say that the Wheel of Time is of vital importance for the world of today, because there is a particular link between Shambala and the world in which we live. The fact is that the Dalai Lama, who is undoubtedly one of the great Tibetan masters, has given this powerful initiation more than twenty times. The first initiation took place in Tibet, in 1954, and there have been more recent ones, in December 1994 in Barcelona and in Mungod in India in January 1995. This was to prepare the future, even if, as he told me, "Shambala remains for me too an enigmatic or even paradoxical land. It is not an ordinary place, more a state of mind or awareness, which can only be lived or experienced according to the individual karmic bonds."

It is true that the history of Shambala and the teachings of the Kalachakra strongly suggest, in the course of the vision of development, the stages in the quest for self-knowledge. However, it is pointless to try and speed up the process: the journey to Shambala is also about learning the importance of giving time to time, in this quest that is intended to take one to the limit of oneself, in order then to return with a spark of wisdom that the masters claim enables one to live in the light of death. There are, however, a few witnesses, very few it is true; their presence and individual experience vouch for it: you must know how to listen to them…

At Leh, in Ladakh (northern India), in 1988: the Dalai Lama begins to create a Kalachakra mandala.

Traditional mandala, on *thangka*, dedicated to the deity
Samksipa Kula Panjara, 83.5 x 74 cm, mid-fourteenth
century. (Private collection.)

# Colored Powders and Computer-Generated Images

Sylvie Crossman

While the Kalachakra Mandala is one of the most complex, it should be remembered that rather than "one" mandala there are "many" mandalas. According to Dagpo Rinpoche there are several hundreds of them. They all can lead to Awakening, but their central figures may vary while always being a manifestation or metamorphosis of the state of Buddhahood. The state of Buddhahood may take on different appearances: some have the face of a real character who has existed in the real world, such as Shakyamuni, the historical Buddha who in the sixth century BC succeeded in reaching Enlightenment, while others have a mythical appearance, like the five major Buddhas of Tibetan Buddhism.

The same Buddha is sometimes represented figuratively (the body mandala), sometimes symbolized by a "seed syllable" (that is, its acoustic form corresponding to the speech mandala) or by the attributes that characterize him (the wheel, the diamond, or the lotus, corresponding to the mind mandala). As well as the mandalas made from colored powder, there are some made from butter, grains of rice, clay, or wood. The majority are painted on fabric, in which case they are known as mandalas on thangka; this is the case with the Kalachakra, which is also painted on the walls of the temple dedicated to him in Dharamsala.

Some mandalas are sculpted, and they may be as large as actual palaces or monasteries; indeed, the monastery of Samyé, built in the eighth century and the first in Tibet, follows the shape of the mandala. One might liken Mount Kailash itself, with its square base and height of 22,028 feet, to a mandala. Considered to be the axis of the world and associated with Mount Meru, the desert-like high plateau of Chang Tang that leads to it is lined with "happiness scarves," scattered on the ground as offerings by the pilgrims traveling to this holy mountain.

Like the people who raised this art to its zenith, the mandala has demonstrated a remarkable ability to adapt to changing times and the vicissitudes of history.

In the prosperous Tibet of the past, mandalas were made from crushed precious stones, or carved from rubies, gold, or turquoise, reflecting the splendour of the rich patrons who, like the patrons of the Italian Renaissance, commissioned these works of art so as to offer them to the great lamas and thus ensure their protection. Today, in the exiled communities in India, Bhutan, Sikkim, and Nepal, the stones and the monasteries themselves are much poorer: there are no more precious stones, either solid or crushed, but instead synthetically colored powder made from rocks found near the rebuilt monasteries are used to make ephemeral Kalachakras.

The most important point is that the mandala should be effective, acting on the subtle areas of the consciousness. It is said that the most experienced disciples need neither colors nor powders to meditate and reach the land of Buddhas. They need nothing beyond the unbreakable certainty of their mind. Their mandalas are visions, inner constructions that are colored by the mere intensity of their concentration.

The journey to the achievement of this level of perfection is a long one and, in the meantime, one has to live in one's own time. Buddha never preached the renunciation of worldly experience; rather he encouraged his disciples to experience the universe of phenomena, to look down into precipices, to experience terror and even lust: it is necessary to experience what one must overcome.

So, just as Aboriginal initiates in Australia today store the sacred motifs determining the tribe they belong to in the memory of their portable computers, Pema Losang Chogyen, a monk at the monastery of Namgyal in Dharamsala in India, traveled to the United States in 1990 to work in the Program of Computer Graphics at Cornell University, in Ithaca, New York.

## A Fluorescent Labyrinth

An artificial intelligence mandala: this is what Pema Losang Chogyen and research scientists of this American laboratory—Donald Greenberg, James Ferwerda, Paul Wanuga, Benjamin Trumbore and Timothy O'Connor—succeeded in producing after working together for a year. A journey through meditation time, when the flat disc of the mandala suddenly acquires form and relief, and becomes a fluorescent labyrinth that the eye follows to the very center. There the objective, the central deity, suddenly appears. In this case it is the terrifying Vajrabhairava[1] symbolized by a blue syllable, erected like a contemporary sculpture. Then one's gaze strikes the forehead of a monk in a dark red habit meditating on the lawn of a campus: hitting the dot or chakra of the forehead, right between the eyes; in this way the mandala penetrates the consciousness of the disciple.

In April 1991, the Dalai Lama, the first lama of the Namgyal Monastery, visited the laboratory and watched the computer-generated mandala. He thought it was wise, and efficient, to resort to a technology capable of expressing the true nature of the mandala as a three-dimensional figure, a palace with levels, and a dynamic path.

He approved the work.

1. Vajrabhairava (literally "Terror of diamond") is the deity that appears in the center of this computer-generated mandala. Also known by the name of Yamantaka, she is usually surrounded by twelve other deities, all of them emanations from the central couple. If, in a moment of extreme clairvoyance, Manjusri, the *bodhisattva* of Wisdom, has taken this particularly menacing aspect—that is, the face of death itself—this is to confront, in his kingdom of shadows, Yama, the lord of death, whose cruelty he judged too detrimental to men. The spectacle of his own ferocity, infinitely magnified, terrified Yama so much that he was overcome: not killed but reduced to nothingness, transformed into his opposite, that is to say into a protective deity endowed with eternal life.

Still from a computer animation of the Kalachakra Mandala
created by Pema Losang Chogyen in collaboration with the
Program of Computer Graphics, Cornell University.

# Thoughts on Tantric Buddhism

Anne-Marie Blondeau

Tantric Buddhism is not a form of religion independent from primitive Buddhism but rather a development of it, a continuation of the successive stages of evolution that Buddhism has undergone since its foundation in the sixth century BC. At the start of the Christian era, original Buddhism developed new forms described by its followers as the "Greater Vehicle" (*Mahayana*) Buddhism, because it offered an altruistic soteriology or doctrine of salvation, in contrast with the quest for deliverance for oneself, the objective of primitive Buddhism, which was by contrast and somewhat pejoratively known as the "Lesser Vehicle" (*Hinayana*) Buddhism. Tantric Buddhism is the ultimate development of the "Greater Vehicle." So there is no antagonism between these different forms; their fundamental doctrine remains identical. Rather there is a transformation of a philosophy and a path to freedom, achieved through reflection and meditation on the nature of things, within a soteriological religion, appealing to compassion and based mainly on cult and rituals.

To make it easier to understand, chronological reference points for the different stages of Buddhism have been established. The Greater Vehicle dates from about the second century AD, Tantrism from the fifth or sixth centuries with the appearance of the first texts, the *tantra*, which gave the movement its name. But the seeds of the Greater Vehicle were already present in some schools of the Lesser Vehicle, while yoga, for instance, which is one of the basic techniques of Tantrism, appeared well before it. Furthermore, these three forms are not mutually exclusive: they have coexisted in time and space, and sometimes even within the same monastery.

To be more precise, Buddhism as it was originally preached by its founder, Gautama, the Buddha Shakyamuni, who was born in the second half of the sixth century BC, offered a long, arduous path towards deliverance from the suffering inherent in all existence. He advocated self-control, asceticism, reflection, and meditation to cast off one's ego, in order to attain Enlightenment, the knowledge of nature, impermanent and

59

devoid of all "existing," in order finally to enter *nirvana*, "the extinction" of all phenomena. This was a long process, carried out over numerous successive lives, and one which was reserved to a few exceptional beings among those who had embraced the monastic life. Laymen, on the other hand, could only hope to improve their *karma*—the burden of the actions of all their previous lives—by accumulating merit (particularly through gifts to the clergy), in order to be reborn in a life in which they would be monks. Soon after Buddha's death, the first signs of the development heralding the Greater Vehicle were seen. For example, the worship of relics began, and thus of the Buddha himself: the communities and the kings who had supported him in India argued over his relics, which they shared among them. Monuments or *stupa* were erected to house these relics. Then gradually, two or three centuries after his death, Buddha began to be represented by images and statues, whereas in the past he had only been indicated by symbolic signs such as the wheel with eight spokes or footprints. A cult emerged, and the sites where Buddha had lived became places of pilgrimage. As the figure of the founder became blurred by the passage of time, it became clothed in legends. The events of his life were transformed into fabulous stories, and the perfect career of this being who was destined to achieve Enlightenment (*bodhisattva*) was retold in the form of edifying stories. These showed how in the course of his previous lives, whether animal or human, he had accumulated wisdom and merit through the practice of Buddhist virtues, particularly compassion, thus enabling him to achieve Enlightenment in this life, becoming Buddha, "the Awakened one."

## The Gods "who have gone out of this world"

It can undoubtedly be said that from then on Buddhism was a religion in the eyes of the faithful. It became more firmly established as such with further developments, which however revealed a radical dichotomy between the Buddhist pantheon and the cult surrounding it, and doctrinal developments. Buddhism is anchored in a sociological reality and is involved in the religious movements that have shaken the Indian continent. People are still debating the influences that affected Buddhism and led to the Greater Vehicle, trying to understand which of the two, Hinduism or Buddhism, influenced the other.

However that may be, one can see in Hinduism the development of a movement that is also present in Buddhism, namely that of worship, *bhakti*. In addition, Buddhism has borrowed whole sections of its culture from Hinduism, whether it be cosmology, the sciences, or the pantheon of gods. This pantheon was incorporated in a category of gods "of this world," vassals of the Buddhas and bodhisattvas who themselves have "gone out of this world." It is they who are worshipped. While the historic Buddha has gradually become deified, numerous Buddhas and bodhisattvas have flourished who no longer have any historical reference but who are endowed with a cosmic character, each governing a "pure" and "heavenly" world. The concept of the bodhisattva has itself changed, showing more

Page opposite:
Romio Shrestha,
contemporary Nepalese
painter, *Mandala of
Vajrasattva* (detail),
1992. (Private
collection.)

clearly the difference between the Greater and Lesser Vehicles from the point of view of beliefs and practices. It no longer refers to a being who in a distant past had decided to reach the state of Enlightenment and achieved it after countless lives. Bodhisattvas are now looked upon as beings who have achieved Enlightenment and, like the Buddha, have crossed the ten stages of the journey to Enlightenment. But then instead of expressing the final wish: "I want to pass into Extinction," they decide not to, out of compassion for others. Indeed, they vowed at the beginning of their careers not to pass into Extinction until all living beings had achieved deliverance. The ideal figure is therefore not that of the Buddha who strives for himself alone but that of the bodhisattva, and the cardinal virtue is the disinterested compassion that leads the bodhisattva to take on all the forms and all the means needed to save living beings. (In Tibetan Buddhism, human beings are considered to be temporary emanations of these great entities.) This led to the birth of new texts, *sutra*, or Sayings of the Buddha, dedicated to one or other of these Buddhas or bodhisattvas. Laymen who have no hope of achieving Enlightenment during this lifetime turn to them and worship them in the hope of being reborn in their "paradise" when they die. In fact, the texts give assurance that the simple fact of remembering a particular Buddha or bodhisattva or saying his name on one's deathbed is enough to make the believer appear in front of him and be taken to his "paradise." This clearly shows that Buddhism had become a religion offering salvation, with prayers, offerings, and propitiations, often accompanied by the recitation of the "formula" that synthesizes the deity and his action, his *mantra*.

But it would be wrong to see only this aspect in the Greater Vehicle. The refinements of doctrinal reflection are equally important. First, the teachings left by Buddha and gathered together in the texts known as *sutra* were often elliptical or even contradictory. Secondly, Buddha had refused to answer a number of metaphysical questions. Finally, the *sutra* of the Greater Vehicle, because they appeared much later (in the first and second centuries AD), had to be authenticated by linking them to the preachings of the Buddha, while they amplified and sometimes transformed them. This explains the development of a very important interpretative literature, using the most sophisticated conceptual methods of Indian philosophy, in particular logic. Thus fundamental concepts in the Greater Vehicle were gradually clarified, for instance that of the three "spheres" in which the activity of the Buddhas took place (the Three Bodies of Buddha), or that of the two registers of truth expressed by Buddha: the ultimate truth, which can only be grasped by beings of great spiritual maturity, and relative truth, for those still involved in the cycle of rebirths, the world of *samsara*.

These concepts made it possible to remove the obvious contradiction between the proliferation of deities in the pantheon and the cults associated with their worship, which were linked to relative truth, and the culmination of Buddha's teaching on the impermanence and empty nature of phenomena: the doctrine of Emptiness. Today the latter is the cornerstone of Buddhism, including its tantric developments. Explained in the Greater Vehicle *sutra* of "The Perfection of Wisdom" that made its appearance in the late first or early second century, it became the objective to be reached, the ultimate Knowledge, the Supreme Body of the Buddha: the Body of the Law. The interpretation and discussions on the nature of Emptiness have given rise to some of the most profound concepts in Buddhist thinking as well as movements and schools in the Greater Vehicle. One of them, which made its appearance during the second half of the fourth century, went so far as to claim the unreality of all phenomena, as the mere products of the intellect, itself polluted by the burden of

Left:
Romio Shrestha, contemporary Nepalese painter, *The Position of Intimate Union* (detail), 1992. (Private collection.)

previous acts. To rid oneself of these and achieve pure knowledge, it advocated yoga techniques to support meditative methods.

It was perhaps among the disciples of this school that Tantrism first developed, but as in the case of the Greater Vehicle, the emergence of Tantrism was diffuse and cannot be dated or placed precisely. Here too, a similar development in Hinduism was apparent. Compared to previous approaches, the great novelty of Tantrism was to offer a quick route to deliverance in this life. Even if it is sometimes expressed in different terms, the doctrinal foundation remains identical and only the means are different: using yoga techniques, external and internal, it is a matter of experiencing an awakening, an intuitive grasp of Reality (that is Emptiness), which causes the individual to pass from the phenomenal to the noumenal level. The novelty is this: Tantrism takes man as he is, making use of his tendencies and passions, while even the Greater Vehicle required several lives of effort to eradicate these components in his personality and achieve control of the mind. In this case control of the mind is presupposed, in that it must have been cleared of the impure activities of the reasoning mind in order to make room for the intuitive grasp—in other words the mystic experience—of Reality, that is the non-duality of the phenomenal world that revolves in the wheel of rebirths, and the Absolute, Emptiness. A quick journey, then, but wisely only reserved for those beings who have achieved the greatest spiritual maturity, the others being obliged to continue their journey along the paths of the two other Vehicles.

# Each Individual is at a Different Stage
# on the Road to Enlightenment

These new methods are based on fundamental texts, the *tantra*, whose original meaning refers to weaving: the shuttle or the warp of cloth. The choice of the name probably refers to the continuity in the transmission that is one of the main characteristics of Tantrism, as will be seen later, and at the same time to the radical unity of the microcosm or macrocosm, the human mind and the Mind-in-itself, the phenomenal and the noumenal. The *tantra* form a collection of heterogeneous texts that touch on a wide range of subjects, from magic rituals (such as calling upon a minor deity to drive away or destroy an enemy), to doctrinal texts, praise of a Buddha or a bodhisattva, or his formula, even rituals accompanying the construction of a monastery. They also include practical instructions, "methods of fulfillment" (*sadhana*), revealed to the great "realized" masters (*siddha*) who have transmitted them. The *tantra* themselves belong to the revealed literature, their appearance dating back to between the seventh and the twelfth centuries. They further developed the use of esoteric formulae, *mantras*, to the extent that Tantrism is also known as the "Vehicle of the *mantra*." The correct enunciation of mantras endows them with them power and effectiveness, whether it be to evoke the gods, to encourage them to act, or to move from the phenomenal to the transcendental level. In short, they are used to "realize" one's goal.

The great diversity of the *tantra* is explained by the same doctrinal justification as the practices of the Greater Vehicle. Each individual is at a different stage in his journey to Enlightenment, and it is a matter of moving forward from the point where one is; to each according to his needs and possibilities, hence these methods range from the seemingly "lowest" levels to the dizzy heights of mystic effusion. The "realized" being who has experienced the non-duality of the phenomenal world (*samsara*) and of *nirvana*, or Emptiness, can use methods that the ordinary person would consider barbaric, disgusting, and against nature, but whose objective always remains highly spiritual (in theory at least). The amalgam of these rituals sometimes associated with black magic can also be explained historically by the fact that Buddhism has never been a unified church—which would have ensured the dogma and orthodoxy of the practices—but a juxtaposition of communities. This tendency reaches its peak in Tantrism whose masters live, surrounded by their disciples, in hermitages or "in the world," but mostly outside the communities of ordained monks. It is therefore easy to understand the numerous influences that affected them, including the elements that were introduced, accepted, and digested having been borrowed from Indian religions, whose rituals go back to the dawn of time, or from indigenous religions supplanted by Buddhism.

In the case of both Hindu and Buddhist *tantra*, their vast number and varied nature quickly made it necessary to arrange them in a certain order and classify them, the criteria being the goals sought and the methods used. There are several classifications that more or less overlap. The

THOUGHTS ON TANTRIC BUDDHISM

classification adopted by the Gelugpa School in Tibet includes four main categories, ranging from the "lowest" to the "highest" as follows:

1. Those that are based on the ritual acts (*kriya-tantra*) using external supports: paintings or images. The goals associated with these *tantra* are divided into four ritual acts: appeasing hostile forces, increasing power and riches, subjugating and destroying enemies—of the doctrine, as a rule. Also included in this category are the "technical" *tantra*, such as those explaining how to make mandala or build a monastery.

2. Those that deal with the conduct of the disciple (*carya-tantra*). These use external supports but also mentally created ones, sometimes even using yoga. The difference between this and the previous category is not obvious and appears to depend on the deity who reveals the *tantra*. The goal to be reached is always connected with action in the phenomenal world.

3. Those that encourage the union with the transcendental using psycho-physiological methods of yoga (*yoga-tantra*): the ritual is interiorized, while the deity who presides over it is visualized, with or without external support, with or without a mandala.

4. The "supreme" tantras (*anuttara-tantra*) that, using the same techniques, deal with the complete process of the evocation of the deity from Emptiness, his incorporation and his reabsorption into Emptiness. Here Emptiness is considered to be the indissoluble union of the saving Means and the Knowledge.

# The Union of Male and Female Principles, of Sperm and Blood

In the western world, Tantrism has long been considered a deviant form of Buddhism with obscure, secret practices. Today, people prefer to call it "esoteric Buddhism," which it effectively is. The secret is on two levels: the incommensurable secrets regarding the state of Buddha, which the ordinary man cannot even contemplate, and practices that the disciple must keep secret so that they are not corrupted by unauthorized individuals. The tantric tradition is in fact based on oral transmission from master to disciple, uninterrupted since the very first revelation. Without this authentic transmission, the reading of the *tantra* and their application based on "realization methods" would be ineffective, and at the worst would lead to perverted practices and views, which would be dangerous. As a result, the master custodian of tradition, the Guru, is the key character, placed in front of the Buddha during invocations. He chooses his disciple, who also chooses him, each one recognizing the bonds that joined them in their previous lives. From this moment onwards the disciple must submit body and soul to his master, promising absolute obedience and trust, sealed by the commitments he has undertaken. One of these commitments is never to reveal anything about the teachings he has received. These teachings are given by the master according to the personality and spiritual progress of the disciple, whom he follows step by step and whom he subjects to the successive initiations that will enable him to advance on the

path to Realization. This necessity for secrecy is reflected in the texts by coded writing that always leaves some doubt as to their meaning, real or metaphorical. This code enables followers to communicate among themselves without being understood by outsiders. Another aspect of Tantrism that greatly shocked the first western experts who became interested in Buddhism was its sexual component, present in both the texts and the iconography. It should be pointed out that this aspect only exists in the final category of the *tantra*, the supreme *tantra*. Here, as mentioned earlier, Emptiness, the Buddha state, is conceived as the realization of the inseparable union of the Means peculiar to Buddha and transcendental Knowledge. Pursuing the cosmological and metaphysical reflection involved in the Greater Vehicle, this system develops a whole play of symbolic and sexual correspondences. In it the means are the god, the male principle, the Sun, sperm, the disciple, while the Knowledge is the consort represented in carnal embrace with the god, the moon, blood, the female partner of the disciple.[1] In the constantly repeated affirmation of the non-duality of the *samsara* and *nirvana*, of the identity of the microcosm and macrocosm, the disciple must experience—a keyword in Tantrism—the union of Means and Wisdom within his own body. The symbolic correspondences are continued here in the psycho-physiological concepts of yoga: the two channels situated to the right and left of the central channel are male and female respectively. Crudely, the technique consists in causing a drop, situated in the forehead, to descend through these two channels. Reunited in a vital center situated above the pubis, it forms the union of the male and female principles, of sperm and blood, and this drop is then caused to go up again through the central channel. The disciple then experiences the union of the Means and Wisdom, he is the god in union with his partner, in a state that again uses a sexual vocabulary: the Great Bliss that is the luminous Emptiness.

Naturally, the interpretation of these texts opens the door to all kinds of hypotheses. According to some schools, the techniques described are purely spiritual and the language is symbolic. According to others they are very concrete and require the presence of a female partner. There are, it is true, some very detailed texts ranging from criteria governing the choice of the right partner to the personal initiation of the woman and the disciple by the master. But here too, the language is so deliberately symbolic that it can only lead to different interpretations depending on the place and time. However that may be, the absolute rule is that the follower must not on any account lose himself to lust or the pleasure of the senses but achieve a "union without desire," retaining the sperm.

As can be seen, Tantrism is far from being a mixed bag of magic recipes and erotic practices. Although it includes a lot of dross accumulated through the centuries as a result of its contact with all kinds of communities, in its highest forms it represents a global vision of the universe, an attempt at communion or fusion with the transcendental, the ultimate meeting point of all great religions of the world.

1. Some *tantras*, including the Kalachakra and others, associate the Sun with the female and the Moon with the male.

Romio Shrestha, contemporary Nepalese painter, *Buddha and his Consort* (detail), 1992. (Private collection.)

Tibetan landscape.

# Inside Tibet

Jean-Claude Carrière

The mandala is a territory. It is defined, on a wall or on a floor, by precise lines. Defined, and moreover without limits, because this territory unceasingly extends itself and overtakes itself. One could say that it is not self-contained, that it divides itself by uniting itself, and that is closes itself in order to open. It touches everything.

I ask myself quite often whether Tibet is not a mandala. That it is a territory, geographically marked on all the maps in the world, no one doubts. That this territory can be invaded, maltreated, and disfigured, is shown by the evidence. People even go so far as to deny it, to proclaim its disappearance (like the mandala that one suddenly destroys, leaving only sign and memory).

It seems to me that all these physical maneuvers do not in any way lead to the pure and simple disappearance of Tibet. Like the mandala—whose proportions are not significant, in the scale of the universe—it prolongs itself, it branches out, it reaches other territories, and it rises above all resonances and images.

Here perhaps—where the people rate the life of the spirit most highly—is a new form of kingdom, escaping from the idea of the nation, the frontier, and even from history. Could it be the "true kingdom," this territory where there would be only masters, which we have been dreaming about for a long time? On the geographical disappearance—the unachievable fact—is also superimposed, year after year, an invisible, invulnerable expansion. We no longer have the passport for Tibet: but Tibet has come to us. We are putting a little of Tibet in each of us. So we become, at the interior or the exterior of the mandala (these two notions have also become merged), partisans, sharers and, to be precise, compatriots.

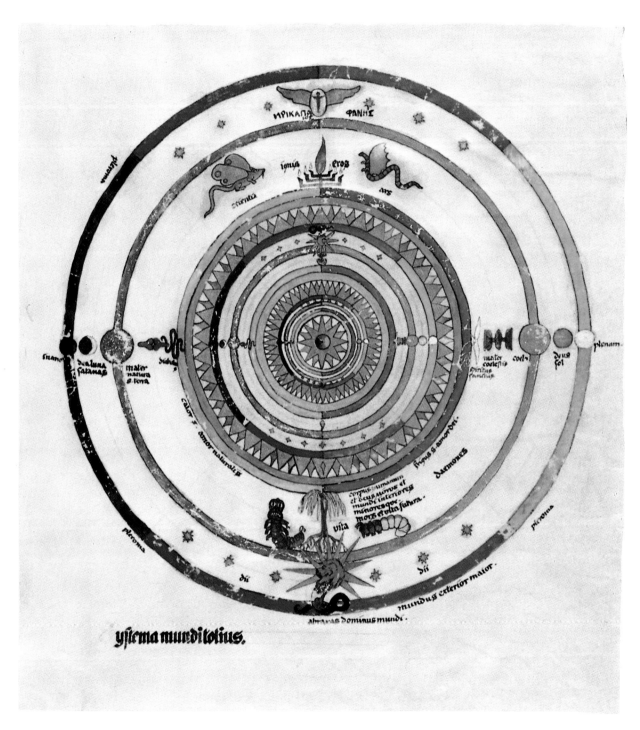

*Systema munditotius* (1916) is recognized as Jung's first mandala; in his commentary on it he said in particular: "This figure depicts the antinomies of the microcosm in the macrocosmic heart of the world that also has its own antinomies. Right at the top, the young boy in the winged egg is called Erikapaios or Phanes, this is a spritual figure evoking the orphic gods. His pendant, right at the bottom, in the world of shadows, has the name Abraxas. It represents the lord of the physical world and is an ambivalent creator. The tree of life takes its roots in this individual to which corresponds, in the upper part of the mandala, the tree and the light in the form of a seven-branched candlestick with these words: *ignis* (fire) and *eros* (love)." In C. G. Jung, *Word and Image*, edited by Aniela Jaffé, Bollingen Series XCVII, Princeton University Press, 1979, p. 2. (© Heirs of C. G. Jung.)

# The Mandala, a Symbol of the Psyche in the Life and Work of C. G. Jung

Ysé Masquelier

## The Mandala Appears in the Life of Jung

In 1913, Jung was 38 years old and his career was at its peak. Since 1905, the head doctor at the Zurich Psychiatric Clinic and Professor at the University had been exchanging ideas with Freud on all the subjects that were opening up with dizzying speed to the explorers of the human soul in the early twentieth century. He had a wife, five children, and numerous patients in private consultation. In 1908 he organized the first international congress on psychoanalysis, and in 1912 he gave a successful series of lectures in New York. He had already written *The Association Experiment*, *Essays on Analytical Psychology*, and *A Study of the Transformations and Symbolism of the Libido*. But this success precipitated the break-up with Freud and failed to prevent the emergence of serious internal, unresolved conflicts in his personal life. He identified the almost ethical need to renounce his elevated position in order to turn himself inwards, if he wanted to continue to support other people. "I could not expect my patients to begin what I had not dared to do myself," he said later.[1]

In 1913, he began an internal journey that might have ended in serious psychosis. His behavior became strange. He distanced himself from his friends, he left his teaching responsibilities to pick up stones on the edge of Lake Zurich, he constructed miniature villages, and he engraved esoteric Latin phrases with a burin. He had dreams in which figures from the unconscious appeared to him, "Elijah," "Salome," and "Philemon," archetypal figures with whom his sick self communicated. This lasted for

Left: C. G. Jung

1. *Memories, Dreams, Reflections*, New York, 1963.

71

nearly three years, and it was towards the end of this long nocturnal cross-
ing that he began to draw mandalas, without knowing what this meant, nor
that he was following a path cleared by others before him, in both the
West and the East. "I painted the first mandala in 1916, after writing the
*Seven Sermons to the Dead*. Naturally, I did not understand it."[2]

2. *Ibid.*

With the mandala, as well as other psychological practices, he began
to find the means to reconstruct himself. Apart from any artistic consideration, drawing became a support for introspection, a "photograph" of his
daily state, and at the same time a prospective image of what he was in the
course of becoming. "In 1918–19, I was at Château-d'Oex as commander
of the English Region of War Internees. There, every morning, I sketched
in a notebook a little drawing in the form of a circle, a mandala, that seemed
to correspond to my interior situation. Enlightened by these images, I
could see day by day the psychic transformations that were operating
within me... It was only gradually that I discovered what a mandala really means: 'Formation, Transformation, Eternal Mind's eternal creation,'"
said Jung, quoting *Faust Part II*.[3]

3. *Ibid.*

For ten years, drawings and paintings of circles, squares, labyrinths,
dark or shining centers of all kinds kept recurring, the unspooling of a
film of an internal process of centering and healing the breaks in his personality. But all this was still very empirical and intuitive, and Jung still
needed to construct a theory based on his own singular experience. This
would allow him to apply an objective interpretation to the dreams or imag-
inations of his patients. The theory, or rather the hypothesis, would be
that the mandala represented the totality of the soul, both conscious and
unconscious, that its center would reveal the existence of an authority much
larger than the ego, the source of psychic life and instigator of its development and its total fulfillment. Later, borrowing from the vocabulary of
India, Jung called this authority the "Self," from the Sanskrit *atman*. But
during the 1920s he felt extremely isolated; he could only find parallels to
what he was experiencing in the spiritual adventures of gnostics or
alchemists, far from the scientific spirit of his times.

## The Secret of the Golden Flower

In 1928, light appeared at last: his friend, the great orientalist Richard
Wilhelm, sent him the translation of a treatise of Taoist meditation, *The
Secret of the Golden Flower*, and asked him if he would prepare a psychological commentary that would make this text more accessible to western
readers. In his autobiography Jung declared that he literally "devoured" the
manuscript, and that he was filled with joy, because this text "brought [him]
an unsuspected confirmation concerning the mandala and its ambulation
round the center. This was the first event that had pierced my solitude. I
felt there a connection to which I could reattach myself."[4] In his introduction to the commentary and Wilhelm's translation, he developed three
strong ideas. First, Chinese wisdom is a dynamic exercise of complimen-
tarity and mediation between opposites. Secondly, the overcoming of conflict is part of the natural development of the psyche, as long as the ego is

4. *Ibid.*

not opposed to "Tao." Finally, and consequently, the correct psychic attitude consists in an acceptance of this process of transformation, in which the ego loses its sovereignty in favor of a more global entity, emerging progressively from the unconscious, and that is the Self. The mandala, in its "crude" forms (dreamed, imagined, invented) or traditional ones (canonical, imposed) simultaneously expresses and accomplishes the mediation between the polarities, the cyclical resolution of the imbalance between the extremes, and the recentering of the psychic energy on the Self.

In an essay entitled "My meeting with C. G. Jung in China," published in the *Neue Züricher Zeitung* in 1929, Richard Wilhelm noted: "The correspondence between Jung's thinking and the wisdom of the Far East is not at all fortuitous. It is in fact the result of profound similarities in their concepts of life. So, it was no coincidence that, coming from China and filled with the most ancient Chinese traditions, I found in the person of Dr. Jung a European with whom I could discuss these questions as with someone who shared a similar framework of references. The following explanation presents itself. Independently of one another, the Chinese sages and Dr. Jung have reached the foundation of mankind's collective psyche, and there they have discovered living elements that are similar because in fact, they actually exist. This seems to prove that the truth can be achieved from different points of departure, provided that one digs deep enough, and that the correspondences between the thoughts of the Swiss researcher and that of the old Chinese sages only serve to demonstrate that they are both right because both of them have discovered the truth."[5]

Jung repeatedly mentioned the upheaval that the introduction of Far Eastern thought provoked in his personal life and medical practice, since after investigating Chinese thought he studied Hinduism and Tibetan Buddhism in depth. In a lecture he gave in memory of Wilhelm, who died in 1930, he highlighted the special nature of this event: "It was there that the spark was produced from which the light was to emanate that would become one of the most meaningful events in my life... There we touched an Archimedean point that could unsettle our western spiritual approach."[6] At the same time, he stopped drawing mandalas. The process of unification and psychic expansion that they had revealed, expressed, and stimulated, had become conscious, and these motions from the unconscious, in the shape of dreams, visions or impulses that could be painted, took another course.

## The Mandala, Symbol of the Soul

In 1930, Jung gave a seminar on the mandala in Berlin. There he produced patterns drawn by the patients, next to Tibetan and Chinese images, a Navajo sand painting, and medieval alchemical manuscripts. He returned to this research in *Psychology and Alchemy* (Zurich, 1944), based on a series of 400 dreams, from which he extracted and commented on the most significant stories. The "patient with 400 dreams" had in fact a predilection for images in the shape of mandalas in all their possible forms:

5. C. G. Jung, *Word and Image*, edited by Aniela Jaffé, Bollingen Series XCVII, Princeton University Press, 1979, p. 94.

6. C. G. Jung, *Commentary on The Secret of the Golden Flower*, Routledge & Kegan Paul, London, 1957.

a serpent that describes a circle; a blue flower; a red ball; a globe; a pendulum; a target; a watch balance wheel; a symmetrical garden with a fountain in the middle; complicated ceremonies in a square space; a wheel with eight spokes; a diamond; a geometrical construction; a circle with a green tree at its center; a fountain in an enclosed garden; a round bouquet of roses; an egg balanced on a gold ring, and so on. These dreamlike symbols strongly resembled the traditional iconography of the alchemists that Jung had already been studying for twenty years and whose manuscripts he collected. This was curious, since the patient had had no exposure to this field. Through the double reading, that of the psychoanalyst searching for the cure, and that of the historian deciphering the manuscripts that he collected, Jung demonstrated that, through all these mandalas, it was the dreamer's psyche itself that was represented in its totality and truth of the moment. The emphasis was sometimes on the objective of the development, the center, the Self; sometimes on the opposing forces, the struggle of the ego with its shadow; and sometimes on the polarities, *animus* and *anima*.

Such images mark the activation of the archetypes, those great deposits of meaning, the share of the collective unconscious that resides in each individual. In dreams, as in religious experiences or artistic emotion, the archetypes are made to vibrate and rise to the surface of consciousness by messages or symbolic creations: the universal human foundation appears as a specific cultural representation, and takes this shape to give the self a fragment of supplementary meaning. On the subject of mandalas, Jung also spoke of various expressions of a central archetype, of totality, of completeness, and of the unification of opposites.

Even now there are countless definitions and descriptions of central symbols in Jung's work that have still not been the subject of an accurate survey. There is an excellent passage in a study dating from 1950, *Concerning the Symbolism of Mandalas,*[7] in which he compared modern mandalas, that is, those appearing in dream-like states or the active imagination, and traditional mandalas, borrowed in particular from Tibetan Lamaism. After the associations with alchemy, this new field of investigation led him to a better understanding of the meaning and purpose of these designs: "Their basic objective is the intuition of a center of the personality, that is to say of a central point within the soul, to which everything is related, by which everything is ordered, and which at the same time represents a source of energy… This center is neither felt nor thought of as the ego, but rather as being the Self. Although on the one hand the center represents a point situated entirely within, on the other it also includes a periphery or a frame that itself contains everything that makes up the Self, that is to say the pairs of opposing elements that make up the whole of the personality. These include first the conscious, then what is known as the personal unconscious, and ultimately… the collective unconscious of which the archetypes are common to all humanity." So, the mandala is a symbol of the soul, because it is the soul's best representation, in its totality, and not only from the view of the limited ego. Jung tried to see the psychic processes differently from the way they are traditionally seen in the west;

7. C. G. Jung, *Psychology and Orientalism*, first appeared in Volume IX of Gesammelte Werke in 1976, under the title *Über Mandalasymbolik*.

Page opposite: *The Castle*, 1928, the last "European mandala" created by Jung. His own interpretation notes: "All the buildings here open towards the center, represented by a castle with a gold roof. (…) Round the castle, the sun is covered by black and white flagstones. They represent opposites here reunited." In *Psychology and Orientalism*.

he attempted to replace a narrow vision restricted to the only phenomena of personal consciousness or unconsciousness by an approach based on the understanding of the self.

## Mandalas, Sickness and Healing

Unlike traditional mandalas, which follow the canonical models and have undergone a process of objectification that only retains the most significant cultural symbols, spontaneous mandalas express first of all the individual, momentary state of the psyche. They are therefore helpful indications to both the therapist and the patient. In the course of the "healing of the soul," Jung accumulated numerous observations on the occurrence and recurrence of centered figures. He pointed out that they appeared through dreams, visions or imaginary creations, in periods "of dissociation or disorientation."

Emerging from the unconscious, they seem designed to "compensate for the disorder and confusion of the psychic state," particularly in certain stages of neurosis or in schizophrenia. Jung saw in this an "attempt at self-healing by nature," of spontaneous rebalancing of the personality by the archetype of totality. This hypothesis was based on his overall concept of the soul as a system that regulated itself and one which, in the most favorable cases, could by itself achieve a decentering of the ego and a recentering on the Self. These favorable cases, however, are rare: either the development slows down and does not achieve the full realization of its inner destiny; or it must depend on face-to-face meetings with a therapist who can overcome resistance, help avoid the pitfalls of introspection and decipher the apparent meaninglessness of the unconscious.

These spontaneously created mandalas, with their profusion of strange symbols, indicate certain paths to follow: "They sometimes seek to express the whole of the individual personality in its internal or external experience of the world, at other times the essential psychological orientation of the latter."[8] The role of the analyst is mainly to listen and let happen whatever springs up from the central foundation of the soul, all the work of adjusting to life following along the line suggested by this vital impetus of self-realization.

8. In this paragraph, the quotations come from *Die Schweizeische Monatschrift*, XV, 4, Zurich, April 1955, pp. 16–21.

Right:
"European mandala" made by a patient of Jung who, on the subject of this patient, quoted a passage from *Upanishads*: "It (the Self) is also what warms the sun, hidden by the golden egg with a thousand eyes like a fire by another. It is certain that is worth meditating on, it is this which is to be sought out." In *Psychology and Orientalism*.

# Christian Variation: the Labyrinth

Michel Zehnacker

T he Buddha enthroned at the center of the lotus with eight petals turned inwards, as well as the Romanesque Christ in the center of the mandorla, his feet placed on a square, and the rose at the center of the cross (the "Rose Cross"): these are all images to which traditions appeal to evoke the order that is at the basis of chaos and the light that shines in the darkness.

They remind us that these higher states can only be achieved gradually. To penetrate a mandala, to reach its central Buddha, the source of Enlightenment, is to enter into a palace, passing through the gates and the surrounding walls, while divesting oneself of one's original nature in order to return to the primordial order. A similar path, with its highly introspective character, punctuated by exercises, is found in the Christian labyrinth.

The word "labyrinth" is thought to be derived both from the Latin *labrus*, the double-headed ax, or *labrum*, the open ditch dug with this Frankish ax, and from *lapis*, meaning stone or rock. The idea of effort, work, and vigilance in the root *lab* also emerges.

## What is this Labyrinth?

E ssentially, a labyrinth is a network of intersecting routes, some of them having no way out but eventually leading to the center of this bizarre spider's web. It is very likely that this figure resulted from prehistoric caves, as is shown by the Cretan labyrinth, the mythical archetype of all labyrinths, that appears to have been associated originally with a complex of caves in southern Crete. Such places form the link between the world of the living and the world of the dead.

This "first," Cretan, labyrinth is seen on coins dating from the fifth century BC. It appears in both circular and square forms. But in its natural configuration, it has no "cul-de-sac" or dead end; although the route is in a single direction, the way leading to the center includes numerous turns and detours. It would be easy to lose one's way and unknowingly turn back.

According to myth it led Theseus to the Minotaur, a monster with the head of a bull and a mouth filled with the flesh of children. After vanquishing him, Theseus found his way back to the light by following the thread given him by Ariadne, the daughter of Minos, the Cretan king, which he had unwound along the route.

All the labyrinths in our cathedrals are built on this model with routes leading to the center.

At Reims, Chartres, and Amiens, the entrance and exit of the labyrinth are through the same opening, situated to the west. The distinctive feature of the plan is a spiral turning eleven times. Labyrinths with several routes and entrances enabling each person to chose their own way, as was the case with the labyrinth designs of the ancient world, are rare in Christian buildings.

# The Fast Route of the Initiated

These Christian labyrinths are most often circular (like those at Ravenna, Pavia, Sens, and Bayeux) or octagonal (Amiens, Saint-Quentin, and Arras), the octagon being an intermediate form between the square and the circle, the union of heaven and earth. The square is much less common. Two unusual variations are the labyrinth at Reims, an octagonal shape with four smaller octagons at its NE, SE, NW and SW corners, and the one at Nuremberg, which is triangular.

The most remarkable labyrinth is at Poitiers. On the north wall of the cathedral is a graffito, a kind of diagram of an oval-shaped labyrinth

The Cretan labyrinth.

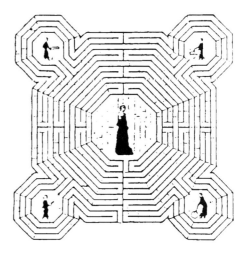

The labyrinth of Reims Cathedral.

that is perhaps a replica drawing by the builder of a labyrinth now destroyed. What is notable is that the Poitiers labyrinth has three entrances: one of them enables the center to be reached directly; the second also reaches the center but only after substantial detours and circumvolutions; the third leads to a dead end.

So as well as the route without an exit, this labyrinth consists of two routes. That which anyone can follow is long and difficult, demanding patience and vigilance. The other, the fast route leading directly to the center, is reserved for the initiated, the mystic.

As for the "eye" of the labyrinth, its center, it usually consists of a brass or marble plaque, or a flagstone. Some of these plaques have now disappeared, and it is possible that sometimes there was no special decoration marking the center.

At the heart of the great labyrinth of Amiens, a medallion depicts the architects who participated in building the cathedral. The large central flagstone was in the past inlaid with a bar and a semi-circle, both of gold, representing the rising of the sun over the horizon. But in the majority of cases, there was, or had been, a representation of the legendary struggle between Theseus and the Minotaur. This scene underlines the pagan origin of the labyrinth and clearly shows that, though the myth is not Christian, Christianity has assimilated and reformed it. The Minotaur becomes Satan while Theseus, the soul regenerated by divine grace, triumphs over evil by arriving at the center, that is to say at the celestial Jerusalem.

What is the symbolism of the Christian labyrinth? The first image that the church has given us is a representation of life on earth with all its burden of misery, trials and tribulations. The tortuous routes, fraught with

The labyrinth of Amiens Cathedral      The labyrinth of Poitiers Cathedral      Sketches by the author.

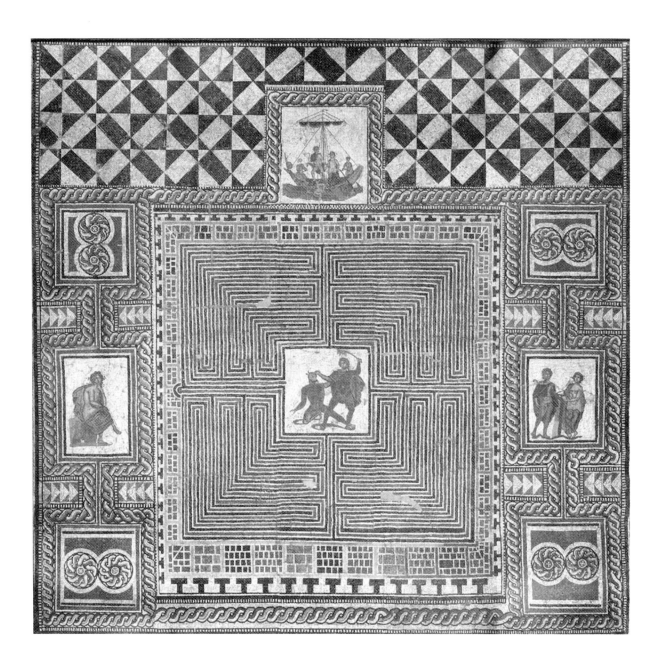

*Theseus Mosaic*, Kunsthistorisches Museum, Vienna.

obstacles and pitfalls, the soul-searching, the long passages in which one can get lost for ever: together they form the image of life held by the Christian of the Middle Ages.

It was this schema that inspired initiatory societies such as the Pythagoreans and the Cathars to devise their own "caves of initiation" in which the candidate for the "Mysteries," having triumphed in all the tests in the darkness, arrived at the center, at the gateway of the sanctuary, and then emerged from the cave as a "new man." The labyrinth, with its perplexing design and its meandering from which there was no escape, represented above all the "Kingdom of the after-life." It had dual symbolism: while the winding passages evoked hell, at the same time they led towards the center, the place of enlightenment. The labyrinth was the path of destiny, the road among the roads, the route between the choice of good and evil, the world of "entrails," "down below," but also the place of the "Mysteries".

## Ariadne, Eros and the Serpent

The thread of Ariadne led, and still leads, to human consciousness. To interpret the symbols underlying the slaying of the Minotaur, it is important to bear in mind that the monster carried the burden of the faults of its mother. He represents not only the destiny of the beast that had to be sacrificed, but also the irruption of bestiality into the human world that, equally, must be punished by death. As for Ariadne, whose thread is sometimes represented by a serpent, she reminds us of the tantric mandala: she is Eros who brings the transfigured, conquering Theseus back towards the Light, after he had left the embodiment of bestiality conquered in eternal darkness. But it was still Eros—Ariadne—who pushed Theseus to enter the labyrinth, who led him to the ultimate hidden caves of our darkest feelings, in order to overcome them.

The Christian labyrinth appears to be inseparable from a whole mythical background. And why should one not think that Theseus killing the Minotaur for love is the prototype of Christ who conquered death and opened the way to life?

Labyrinths were also used as a substitute for the pilgrimage to the Holy Land, since they symbolized the "Road to Jerusalem." Those who were too old or sick to go to the Holy City, the earthly symbol of the perfect city, traveled this "road" on their knees while singing the psalms of David or the *Miserere*.

The pilgrimage itself had an esoteric meaning associated with the idea of the labyrinth, a fact supported by an anonymous fourteenth-century text intended for the members of the Brotherhood of St John, entitled *Seven Instructions to the Brothers of St John*.

"The pilgrim abandons everything and sets off walking towards Jerusalem, which he must perceive as the luminous center of himself and of the regenerated world. He passes through the four corners of the horizon and penetrates the seven domains that are the seven successive states of the pilgrim. From the Kingdom to Grace, this Palace consists of rooms fitted inside each other with their doors and their guardians. During this descent into itself, the body and corruptible soul twice find death and twice they are brought back to life, regenerated. The descent into the seven rooms evokes the interior, and it is indeed through the interior, and through it alone, that the pilgrimage to the Holy Land is possible. This pilgrimage to the inner Jerusalem is illustrated in the sanctuaries by the drawing of the labyrinth on the paving. To reach the center of the labyrinth means that one has followed the route, which has become the way. Thus, we are now at the center."

# The Return to Oneself

In the labyrinth of Chartres, we arrive at the central lobe by the seventh passage, having descended into the various rooms of the labyrinth, passed through the four corners of the horizon, and three times to the East. The similarity is astonishing. It is repeated everywhere, as if the labyrinths had all been designed by the same architect according to the same archetypal plan. One sets out from the West, one forks a first time to the north, the world of origins, in the Middle Ages the domain of Satan and of seduction, to reach in the south the last turning leading to the world of light, bliss, and the purified soul.

Then, the "tests" take on their full meaning. It is necessary to triumph over difficulties several times to find the entrance again, the profane world, where seduction and pleasure dominate. The outcome of the initiatory way depends on this success.

The fact that at Reims and Amiens the master masons memorialized themselves at the center of the labyrinth, at the innermost point of its meanderings, is to emphasize that the labyrinthine route leads to mastery.

The analogy between the master mason of the Middle Ages and the Cretan architect Daedalus is found in the very meaning of the name of this person associated with the legend of Theseus. The name Daedalus comes from *daidallein*, which means "to build cunningly," but it is also a synonym for "skillful". According to legend, Daedalus invented the double-headed ax, the set square, and the spirit level.

So, the labyrinth is indeed the image of the initiatory way, representing a substitute for pilgrimage, the return to oneself, a survival of pagan myths, and a kind of "Golden Book" of the guilds of companion builders.

Today labyrinths have for the most part disappeared, relentlessly removed by the men of the Age of Enlightenment. The Middle Ages had given life and work a holy meaning that did not survive into modern times. But the profound sense of symbolism still survives strongly today: fighting one's own Minotaur, that which devours us from within, looking deeply within oneself, and, at the end of the long and tortuous route, hoping to reach a fragment of Truth and Enlightenment.

# The Kalachakra Mandala
# at la Villette

Jean Audouze

The complex of the park and great hall of la Villette was created to introduce its visitors to the liveliest and most creative cultures of the world through its wide-ranging programs.

The creation of the Kalachakra Mandala in the Tusquets Pavilion in the park of la Villette, which ended with its dispersal in the Canal de l'Oucq, illustrated in a spectacular and exemplary manner the reflections and actions we hope to carry out on this site. We, the visitors, artists, creators, and staff who work on these premises, are constantly made aware of the paradoxes and contrasts of this place, in the same way that Buddhist thought is inspired by the juxtaposition of the precarious and the permanent, of impassivity and compassion.

Such oppositions are evident at la Villette, the urban park consisting of small and large entities, open or closed, mineral or vegetable. Conceived by Bernard Tschumi, the park is based on the arrangement of follies in an enormous regular checker board, with straight paths, and walks that lead the visitor in twists and turns around the various gardens. This park is therefore like a kind of more permanent mandala, marked out by these red points, the follies, that punctuate the proliferation of walks.

The spirit of the mandala is not only present in the layout of this site, which has preserved its historical character while leading the way into the third millennium. It is perhaps particularly present in our conception of the cultural act. Its aim is not to exclude any sector of the creative or thinking process, while suggesting paths of initiation and appropriation to the visitor. The knowledge, the artistic and contemplative development, the simple fact of resting and meeting in this place is fruitful and should lead to a feeling of jubilation and tolerance.

The mandala is not only an artistic geometric construction. It is also one of the manifestations of Tantric Buddhism that proclaims the existence of indestructible links between the past, the present, and the future. Today the enormous urban cultural center of la Villette has been completed at last. It is set in the historical context of its ancient commercial origins—a meat market once existed on the site, of which the large market hall and a few adjacent buildings still remain. But it is also based in the third millennium with the network of communications that it generates between the city's inhabitants and artistic and scientific creation.

In spite of the problems and persecution that it continues to suffer, Tibet opens the way towards the joy of the spirit for us through its mandalas. During these weeks of monastic work, visitors were invited to share their progress towards humility and discovery. Some of us gained a new appreciation for the spiritual richness of the Tibetan people who, through their exile and everything that they have to endure, can teach us in the West that nothing in this universe is without significance and that everything has a meaning, from the smallest grain of sand or color to the stars that illuminate the sky and whose children we are.

# Glossary

**Bardo:** The disembodied state between death and rebirth.

**Bodhisattva:** A being filled with compassion who, on the road to Enlightenment, delays his own accomplishment and becomes reincarnated in order to help others on the journey to Enlightenment.

**Buddha:** Every being who, having achieved Enlightenment, is no longer subject to the cycle of reincarnations. There are countless Buddhas.

There is the **historical Buddha:** Born a prince, under the name Siddhartha Gautama, in northern India in about 527 BC, he disappeared—or entered the final *nirvana*—in about 483 BC. According to tradition, he is also known as Shakyamuni or "Sage of the Shakya clan." This Buddha is considered the Buddha of modern times, the fourth in a long line of future Buddhas.

But there are also **cosmic Buddhas** who, unlike Shakyamuni, never existed and were figures invented by the various schools of Buddhism. Tibetan Buddhism places five of the Buddhas—or *jinas*, victors—at the head of its pantheon. They are Akshobya, Amitabha, Amoghasiddhi, Ratnasambhava, and Vairocana.

Then there are also all the **Buddhas** or **protecting deities**—such as Kalachakra, Buddha of the Wheel of Time—who act as guides for everyone on the path to Enlightenment.

**Compassion:** Sensitivity to the suffering of others and with a desire to alleviate this suffering. This is the key virtue of Tibetan Buddhism. Chenrezi, *bodhisattva* of Compassion, is the patron saint of Tibet.

**Dalai Lama:** "Ocean of wisdom," the Mongolian title given to the head of the Gelugpa order since the seventeenth century, and today the spiritual and temporal leader of Tibet. The Gelugpas, called the "yellow hats" or the "virtuous," are a branch of Tibetan Buddhism. Tenzin Gyatso, the present Dalai Lama, is the fourteenth in the line. Born in 1935 and enthroned in 1940, he fled from his country in 1959 after it had been occupied by Communist China. He now lives in Dharamsala in northern India.

**Deity:** There are two kinds of deities. The "mundane deities" live in our world. They could be described as kinds of spirits or state of minds. The "deities beyond the world" are the forms or emanations taken by the historical Buddha or other Buddhas, according to the temperament of each disciple, in order to teach him in the most appropriate manner.

**Dharma:** The doctrine of the Buddha symbolized by a wheel.

**Enlightenment:** The state achieved by the historical Buddha at about the age of thirty-five years under the pippal fig tree of Bodhgaya in eastern India. This is the state in which the actual, non-dualist, nature of Reality is grasped not as intellectual understanding but as an intuitive perception. In Tibetan Buddhism this supreme knowledge is not achieved without compassion.

**Hinayana:** This is the primitive Buddhism that emerged in the sixth century BC and which the followers of the *Mahayana* (a later development of Buddhism that appeared in the second century AD) pejoratively named the "Lesser Vehicle." The *Hinayana* emphasizes personal salvation. It still survives in Sri Lanka, Burma, and the former Indo-China.

**Kalachakra:** Literally the "Wheel of Time" or "Time Machine," The *Kalachakra Tantra* is one of the methods, one of the liturgical texts—*tantra*—on which Tibetan Buddhism or Tantric Buddhism is based. There are four categories of *tantras*: the *tantras* of Action, Performance, Yoga and Highest Yoga. The *Kalachakra Tantra*, which includes the creation of the mandala of Kalachakra, belongs to the category of Highest Yoga. The Kalachakra is unique in that it contains a very elaborate cosmology, presupposing an apocalyptic vision of history ending with a appallingly barbaric war that will be won the inhabitants of a mysterious kingdom, inhabited by *bodhisattvas* and called Shambala.

**Karma:** Literally "act." The universal law of causality according to which the future of living beings (either in this life or in subsequent lives) is determined by the quality, positive or negative, of their present acts.

**Kata:** A white scarf, a mark of respect and symbol of the purity of feelings, exchanged between a host and his guest, or offered in homage to the statues of deities.

**Lama:** Derived from *la* ("superior," through knowledge) and *ma* ("mother," through compassion), this term echoes the qualities of wisdom and love of the *lama*, spiritual master, monk or layman, versed in the Buddhist doctrine and/or tantric practice.

**Lung Ta:** "Wind Horses." Pennants printed with prayers and drawings of good omen, sent to the gods by the wind. They are found on most buildings and mountain passes in Tibet and in places of exile.

**Mahayana:** The "Greater Vehicle" stresses the impor-

tance of compassion and is based on the ideal of the *bodhisattva* who devotes himself to guiding all beings towards the ultimate deliverance. The *Mahayana* implies that Enlightenment is accessible to laymen, and not only to monks, because the "nature of Buddha" is common to all. Having emerged in India in about the second century AD, it later spread to China, Tibet, Mongolia, Korea, and Japan.

**Mandala:** Symbolic representation, usually highly elaborate, set within a centered disc and used as a support during meditation and initiation.

**Mantra:** Short sacred formula, spoken repetitively out loud or in the mind, enabling one to reach or act on the deeper layers of the mind, while also having psychic effects.

**Mudra:** Like *mantras*, these hand gestures produce psychic responses.

**Nirvana:** Literally "extinction" (of all passion and attachments), the term *nirvana* refers to the passage from the illusory world of phenomena to that of absolute reality or perfect unity. This is the characteristic state of Buddhas who have been definitively delivered from the cycle of deaths and rebirths.

**Potala:** The palace-monastery, built in Lhasa, the capital of Tibet, by the fifth Dalai Lama in the seventeenth century. It was the traditional residence of

the Dalai Lamas from that date until 1959, when the fourteenth Dalai Lama left Tibet, occupied by Communist China.

**Rinpoche:** Literally, "precious." It is the title given to great lamas or recognized incarnations.

**Samadhi:** The state of profound concentration in which existence is directly recognized as being, by its nature, emptiness.

**Samsara:** Literally, "migration." This is the world as it is perceived, unsatisfactorily, by the senses.

**Sangha:** Community of practicing Buddhists in the broad sense of the word, ranging from ordinary laymen to the assembly of *bodhisattvas*, as well as all the monks and nuns.

**Shakti:** The spiritual energy of a given deity, embodied in female form.

**Stupa:** Monument symbolizing Enlightenment, called *chörten* in Tibetan and sometimes used as a funerary monument for high-ranking lamas.

**Tara:** According to legend, Tara was born from the tears of compassion shed by Chenrezi, the patron saint of Tibet. She is one of the twenty-one deities, or symbolic female figures, used as a support in meditation. Two of them, green Tara and white Tara, are the guardian deities of Tibet and Mongolia respectively. Tara's numerous emanations help the practicing Buddhist to cross obstacles on the path to Enlightenment.

**Thangka:** "A thing that one unwinds." The *thangkas* are sacred images made on a roll, using any technique (such as painting, embroidery, or appliqué).

**Truths, Four Noble:** These are the basis of Buddha's teachings, expounded in his first sermon in Benares: the truth about suffering (*dukkha*), the truth about the origin of suffering, the truth about the end of suffering, and the truth about the path leading to the end of suffering. *Dukkha* indeed means "suffering," but it implies even more than that: imperfection, finitude, contingency, impermanence, and vanity.

**Vajra:** *Dorjé* in Tibetan, meaning "lightning" or "diamond;" the emblem of Tibetan Buddhism, it refers to everything that is absolutely pure and indestructible.

**Vajaryana:** This is the "Diamond Vehicle" or the development of the Greater Vehicle in Tibet that dates back to the fifth–sixth century AD. It is also known as esoteric or Tantric Buddhism because it is based on secret, sacred texts, the *tantras*. This school puts the emphasis on compassion that is capable of generating supreme bliss. It uses the artistic imagination—hence the importance of the mandala in Tibet—to achieve Enlightenment in a single life.

**Yab-Yum:** Literally "mother-father;" this is the posture of intimate union adopted by the two deities at the center of the mandalas. It symbolizes the union of wisdom (female) and compassion (male), which generates and characterizes Enlightenment.

**Yoga:** Complex, rigorous practice of a physical and mental discipline that enables the individual to achieve union with the Divine Source.

# Bibliography

## The Universality of Form

Barou, Jean-Pierre, *L'Œil pense, essai sur les arts primitifs contemporains*, Editions Balland, Paris, 1993.

Crossman, Sylvie, *Le Nouvel Age*, Editions du Seuil, collection Points Actuels, Paris, 1981.

Elkin, E. P., *The Australian Aborigines and How to Understand Them*, Sydney, Australia, 1938

Kandinsky, Wassily, *Concerning the Spiritual in Art, New York, 1946*

Klee, Paul, *Théorie de l'art moderne*, Editions Denoël, collection Médiations, Paris, 1964. Zolbrod, Paul G., *Dine bahane': The Navajo Creation Story*, Albuquerque, New Mexico, 1984

## Practice of Mandala

Bryant Barry, *With the Monks of Namgyal Monastery, The Wheel of Time, Sand Mandala, Visual Scripture of Tibet*, Harper, San Francisco, 1992.

Geshe Lhundub Sopa; Jackson, Roger; Newman, John, *The Wheel of Time, the Kalachakra in Context*, Snow Lion Publication, New York, 1991.

Geshe Ngawang Dhargyey, Chö Yog Thubten Jamyang, *Kalachakra Initiation*, Deer Park, Madison, 1981. Hopkins, Jeffrey, Introduction to *The Kalachakra Tantra, Rite of Initiation*, London, 1985.

Tucci, Giuseppe, *Theory and Practice of the Mandala*, New York, 1970

## External Mandala, Internal Mandala

Arguelles, Jose and Miriam, *Mandala*, Berkeley, 1972

Brauen, Martin, *The Mandala: Sacred Circle in Tibetan Buddhism*, Boston, 1997

Dhargyey Geshe Lharampa Ngawang, *A Commentary on the Kalachakra Tantra* (translated by Gelong Jhampa-Kelsang), Dharamsala, 1985.

Hopkins, Jeffrey, Introduction to *The Kalachakra Tantra. Rite of Initiation*, London, 1985.

Imaeda Yoshiro, "Peintures cosmiques du Bouthan," in *Orientalia Iosephi Tucci Memoriae Dicata*, G. Gnoli and L. Lanciotti, Rome,1987.

Kalu Rinpoche, *The Dharma: That Illuminates All Beings Impartially Like the Light of the Sun and the Moon*, Albany, New York, 1986

Lati Rinpoche, Hopkins, Jeffrey, *Death, Intermediate State and Rebirth in Tibetan Buddhism*, London 1979

Mullin, Glenn H., *Selected Works*

*of the Dalai Lama I (Dge 'dun grub). Bridging the Sutras and Tantras*, Cornell University Press, Ithaca, 1985.

**Mus Paul,** "Barabudur : les origines du stupa et de la transmigration", Essay of comparative religious archeology, in *Bulletin de l'Ecole francaise d'Extrême-Orient* (Vol. XXXII, facs. 1, 1932, pp. 269–439; Vol. XXXIII, 1933, p. 577–980).

**Tenzin Gyatso,** *The Kalachakra Tantra, Rite of Initiation, Stage of Generation, A Commentary on the Text of Kay-drup-ge-lek-bel-sang-bo, by Tenzin Gyatso, the Fourteenth Dalai Lama,* translation and introduction by Jeffrey Hopkins, London, 1985.

## The Mandala, a Symbol of the Psyche in the Life and Work of C. G. Jung

C. G. Jung,

*Memories, Dreams, Reflections,* New York, 1963

*Modern Man in Search of a Soul,*New York, 1956

*Man and his Symbols,* New York, 1964

**Serrano, Miguel,** *C. G. Jung and Hermann Hesse, A Record of Two Friendships,* New York, 1965

**Yse Tardan-Masquelier,** *C. G. Jung, la sacralité de l'expérience intérieure,* Droguet-Ardant, Paris, 1992.

## On Tibetan Buddhism in General

*L'Enseignement du Dala'i Lama,* Editions Albin Michel, Paris, 1976.

*Comme un éclair déchire la nuit,* Editions Albin Michel, Paris, 1992.

**The Dalai Lama,** *Cent elephants sur un brin d'herbe.* Editions du Seuil, Paris, 1990.

**The Dalai Lama; Jean-Claude Carrière,** *La Force du bouddhisme.* Editions Robert Laffont, Paris, 1995.

**Blofeld John,** *The Tantric Mysticism of Tibet,* New York, 1970

**Levenson B. Claude,** *The Dalai Lama, A Biography,* New York, 2000

*Ainsi parle le Dalai Lama,* Editions Balland, Pans, 1993.

**Rhie, M. Marylin; Thurman, A. F. Robert,** *Wisdom and Compassion, The Sacred Art of Tibet,* Asian Art Museum of San Francisco and Tibet House, New York, 1991.

**Chogyam Trungpa,** *Cutting through Spiritual Materialism,* Boston, 1973.

# Acknowledgements

This work was originally published in French as *Tibet Roue du temps: pratique du mandala* to accompany an exhibition for the establishment of the Park and Great Exhibition Hall at la Villette in France. Sylvie Crossman and Jean-Pierre Barou were the directors of the exhibition.

Thanks go to Pema Losang Chogyen and the Program of Computer Graphics at Cornell University as well as to James A. Ferwerda of Cornell University. To Daniel Bedos, Martine Bigot Gargar, Jean-Paul Capitani, Jean-Francois Carrère, Sharad Chandra, André Devaux, Michel Déon, Dominique de Leusse, Christine Estève, Michèle and Maurice Galut, Robert Hinshaw, Annick and Jean-Pierre le Ny, Alain Lévy, Gian Franco Lunardo, Pascal Plat.

*Special thanks to:*

*in Dharmasala*, the executive committee of the Namgyal Monastery and Tenzin Geyche Tethong, secretary to His Holiness the Dalai Lama;

*in Basel*, Ulrich Hoerni;

*in Zurich*, Paul Brutsche, director of the C. G. Jung Institute and Maria-Cecilia Röst;

*in Paris*, to the Tibetan Bureau and Dawa Thondup, representative of His Holiness, the Dalai Lama and to Michel Cool; to *Libération*, Michel Vidal-Soubias and Aline Valéro; to *Ateliers Magazine* and Martine César and Frank Schmitt; and to Editions Albin Michel and Jean Mouttapa.

*in Simla*, to lama T. C. Thinley;

*in Barcelona*, to Tibet House and lama Wangchen;

*in Montpelier*, to le Crédit Agricole for its loyal support of Art Sans Frontières.

# Photo credits